Foreign Direct Investment and the Multinational Enterprise

Foreign Direct Investment and the Multinational Enterprise

A Re-examination Using Signaling Theory

SCOTT X. LIU

Foreword by Alan M. Rugman

Westport, Connecticut
London

Library of Congress Cataloging-in-Publication Data

Liu, Scott X.
    Foreign direct investment and the multinational enterprise : a re-examination using signaling theory / Scott X. Liu ; foreword by Alan M. Rugman.
        p.   cm.
    Includes bibliographical references and index.
    ISBN 0-275-95483-8
    1. International business enterprises.   2. Investments, Foreign.
I. Title.
HD2755.5.L558   1997
332.67'3—DC21   96–40533

British Library Cataloguing in Publication Data is available.

Library of Congress Catalog Card Number: 96–40533
ISBN: 0-275-95483-8

First published in 1997

Praeger Publishers, 88 Post Road West, Westport, CT 06881
An imprint of Greenwood Publishing Group, Inc.

Printed in the United States of America

The paper used in this book complies with the Permanent Paper Standard issued by the National Information Standards Organization (Z39.48–1984).

10 9 8 7 6 5 4 3 2 1

Contents

Illustrations

TABLES

Foreword

In this pathbreaking book, Professor Scott X. Liu makes one of the most important contributions to the literature on foreign investment since the 1960 dissertation of Stephen Hymer was published in 1976. He builds upon the transaction costs approach of internalization theory and extends it in a new direction by the use of signaling theory. When there are transaction costs, such as a lack of perfect information or a public goods problem in pricing knowledge, then there is an incentive for internalization within the structure of a firm. Once an international dimension is introduced to transaction costs then internalization takes place within a multinational firm.

In a world of market imperfections, the multinational enterprise (MNE) is the vehicle for internalization, with ownership of foreign subsidiaries being a method for the extension of property rights across national borders. It is not that the equity ownership of subsidiaries by the MNE itself is of value (for example, the nation state cannot appropriate the MNE by nationalization) but rather that the knowledge is an intangible intermediate product embedded in the social structure of the MNE. Economists have noted that the intangible knowledge finds its way into final goods and services sold by the MNE, but there are few (if any) satisfactory methods of decoupling the knowledge from the structure of the MNE. Therefore, we can conclude that the MNE is a package of intangible knowledge inputs, and that internalization theory is a theory of the MNE.

This is the core literature of international business, first developed by Buckley and Casson, with important original insights by Caves, Johnson, Rugman, Hennart, and others. Yet while internalization theory (and Dunning's related eclectic approach) is the dominant paradigm of the international business field, it has been difficult to test due to the core problem of the intangible nature of knowledge. Now can empirical work be done on intangibles? One answer, developed here by Professor Liu, is to analyze the MNE's investment as signals, whose effects are interpreted by other MNEs. In other words, signaling theory provides perceptual insights into the strategies of MNEs, in which firm-level investments and the reactions can be analyzed. This advances internalization theory in a new and potentially more powerful theoretical direction and broadens the ground for empirical research.

Signaling theory comes into play when there are information asymmetries between buyer and seller, that is, when a market cannot be made. As Professor Liu notes in his Preface, Hymer himself diagnosed incomplete information as a reason why foreign direct investment (internalization by the MNE) is preferable to licensing. The MNE's choice of foreign direct investment over licensing is a signal read by other participants in the global economy, and one which the MNE itself understands may convey strategic information.

This book is the first one to integrate signaling theory into the mainstream internalization paradigm of international business. It is full of useful insights and is a valuable contribution to the literature on the theory and operational management of the MNE. As such, it is an indispensable addition to the library of any serious researcher in the field of international business. The high quality of this book will guarantee it a long life.

Alan M. Rugman
University of Toronto

Preface

In 1983 I left my native China for Toronto, Canada, where I joined the public accounting profession and worked for Touche Ross. At that time, China, largely still a mystery to Westerners, was a nation roiled by decades of political turmoil. Mao Zedong had just died; the Cultural Revolution had ended with disgrace; the radical faction, the Gang of Four, had been purged; and many Chinese had become totally disillusioned with what they had experienced. This vast land was facing uncertainty, poverty, and economic stagnation. However, it was also the time when China turned to the path of economic reform and an open-door policy. At that time, nobody would have imagined that in ten years China would arouse the world's attention with its economic upsurge.

Because of my involvement with the World Bank's projects, I have travelled extensively in China during the last two years. Every time I am there, I see something new: around-the-clock construction of buildings, highways, and shopping centers; the Chinese people's aspiration for material consumption and to get rich quick; and cities plagued by traffic congestion and pollution. The whole society is dynamic and rapidly changing. The influence of Western commercial culture is pervasive, with the logos, brand names, and TV commercials of all world-class multinationals everywhere. The noticeable changes started to take place only in the last six or seven years. Because of my vivid memory of the China of not long ago, I often forget that I am not in Hong Kong, Taipei, or Seoul but in Beijing or Shanghai. Now China is the world's second largest recipient of foreign direct investment with a total of $26 billion in 1994, while India, the second most populous country, has only attracted $2.5 billion in foreign capital in the same period. For better or worse, China is a real example of how the multinational enterprise (MNE) and foreign capital and technology can transform a national economy in a short period. It was this observation that provided me with many of the ideas and examples in this book.

When I was at Touche Ross, I became interested in the operations of the MNE, with my job experience dealing with many major multinational enterprises. This interest eventually led to my decision to research the theory of multinational enterprise. On the surface, this research field appears to be a mature area with a well-established body of literature. I still remember my conversation with Professor Calvet, with whom I sat through a session on the new MNE theories during the Academy of International Business conference in 1993. He commented that many of the speakers just repeated the things that had been said over ten years ago. Similar opinions have also been expressed by others (e.g., Bergsten et al. 1978, Kindleberger 1984, McClain 1983). Teece summarizes the existing accomplishment of the research:

In the last decade, there has been a flurry of articles and books on the theory of the multinational enterprise, including Hymer (1970, 1976), Buckley and Casson (1976), Dunning (1981), Teece (1981a,b, 1983), Hennart (1982), Rugman (1981, 1982), and Caves (1982). These works have in common their emphasis on the multinational enterprise as an internalizer of economic activities, in the spirit of Coase (1937) . . . Kindleberger (1984, p.181) claims that virtually all the ideas that have emerged as the "new theories" can be found in Hymer. (1986, p. 21)

This view is further reinforced by Horaguchi and Toyne (1990) in their review of Hymer's work since 1976.

It appeared to be difficult to add more to the current body of research. However, when I dug deeper into the literature, I became convinced that there was a gap, a missing link between the theoretical and empirical research on the multinational enterprise. There was a research issue that deserved further exploration. This conviction led to this book on the signaling framework of foreign direct investment (FDI).

I may well claim that this is the first research on FDI signaling; that is, the first research to explore the perceptual effect of the MNE's foreign investment posture and its implications to the firm's market transactions. However, when I reread Hymer recently, I was struck by one paragraph referring to the obstacles to technology transfer through the market:

In a world of uncertainty there may be a conflict of evaluations, which make cooperation difficult. Business is risky, and businessmen receive signals but not complete information. People read signals differently and so act differently even where their goals are identical. Hence there is a difficulty of reaching an agreement between the licenser and the licensee. The owner of the advantage [namely technological know-how] may use it himself because his evaluation of it is different

from the evaluation of other people because he has more information abut his
advantage and a greater incentive to use it. (1976, p. 50)

Hymer's message is explicit and unmistakable in the text. Given that the
buyer does not have the same access to information as the seller, it is
difficult to organize the transactions of know-how in the market. Although
there are signals in the market, they are not credible. As a result, the owner
of know-how prefers FDI internalization to licensing. I was astonished.
Did Hymer mean that if there were credible signals, the integrity of the
market would be preserved? Would he further consider that after a firm's
choice of FDI internalization, some credible signals might develop in the
market for know-how? These questions cannot be answered because of
Hymer's premature death in 1974. As such, I feel obliged to cite this
paragraph in the preface to remind us of what Hymer perceived over twenty
years ago. Once again, I was totally overwhelmed by his insight and
wisdom.

Acknowledgments

This book would have been impossible without the significant contribution and support of many individuals. Their contribution, stimulation, and encouragement simply cannot be forgotten. First, Chapter 5 is a product of my joint venture with Professor Rachel Baiyang Yang, whose intelligence, insights, and background of rigorous training are impressive and always the source of my admiration. I would like to express my deep gratitude to Dr. John W. Bagby and Dr. Prasad Padmanabhan, whose time, persistence, and suggestions contributed to my research progress. I owe enormous debt to Dr. James C. McKeown, an empiricist in accounting with national fame, and whose timely and thoughtful comments and suggestions led to remarkable improvement in the quality of this work, and to Dr. Eric W. Bond, a distinguished economist whose initial support and instinct gave me the courage to pursue this untapped topic, and whose valuable input is reflected in the whole text. I also would like to thank Dr. John C. Spychalski, the Chair of the Business Logistics Department of the Smeal College of Business Administration at Penn State University for his support. This book is based on research that received the 1993 Richard N. Farmer Competition Award of the Academy of International Business, and I am grateful to the award committee members, Professors Yair Aharoni, Alan M. Rugman, Ravi Ramamurti, and Robert Green, for their recognition of my work.

On numerous occasions, I have received comments, suggestions and support from many scholars, including Alan M. Rugman, John Dunning, Farok Contractor, Alan Calvet, Bernard Yeung, and Kang Ray Cho. To all these individuals, I offer my sincere gratitude. I would like to thank my old friend, Dr. Siehoon Lee of Samsun Company, with whom I shared happiness, frustration, and stress during my graduate study, and whose help to me is too much to mention. I appreciate especially the help of Alan Piazza of the World Bank, who provides me with insights to China's development based on his profound working knowledge and the opportunity to research into its current being. My appreciation also goes to many dear friends and colleagues, including Marsha Konz, Brad Condie, Jon Baum, Peng He, Tracey Leffin-Hedrick, Ray Pan and Henry Sun, whose moral and intellectual support simply cannot be forgotten. I am indebted to all of them for their assistance in the completion of this endeavor.

The highest recognition goes to my parents Professor Liu Hua and Ms. Cao Zhuting, whose love is constant and unfailing and who make me what I now am. Finally, my deepest love and appreciation go to my dear wife, Joane Y. Chao.

Foreign Direct Investment
and the
Multinational Enterprise

1

Introduction

Foreign direct investment (FDI) takes place when a firm acquires ownership control of a business unit in a foreign country. It is attained in the form of either (1) establishing a new subsidiary/branch, (2) acquiring a control share of an existing firm, or (3) participating in a joint venture. This investment extends the firm's corporate network across national boundaries, allowing it to maintain ownership over a package of resources transferred abroad, including capital, equipment, engineering expertise, and managerial and marketing skills. The first U.S. direct investment, for example, happened in 1867, when Singer Sewing Machine Co. set up a plant in Scotland to undertake manufacturing there. This incident symbolized the beginning of Singer's process of multinationalizing its operations, with each subsequent foreign entry further extending the multinationality of the firm.

A relevant question then is "At what stage of foreign expansion has the firm become a multinational enterprise (MNE)?" More specifically, how should the MNE institution be defined? A survey by Aharoni (1971) presented different definitions of the MNE based on different measures, which include (1) structural criteria, such as the number of foreign operations and the multinationality of the owners and management team, (2) performance criteria, such as foreign assets, sales and earnings as percentages of the total, and (3) behavioral criteria, such as the global orientation of the top management. These different approaches reflect the effort to identify the overriding factor which differentiates the multinational firm from the domestic firm. The problem is that, while emphasizing different aspects of the internationality, they are all based on some measures whose cutoff points are subjectively determined. Less controversy would arise if the definition starts with the firm's action which triggers the process of multinationalization. For practical purposes, the multinational enterprise is defined simply as a firm that undertakes foreign direct investment.

The overseas expansion of national firms got under way in the early 1900s. However, it became a prominent event in the world economy in the post–World War II decades, as exhibited by a spectacular growth of direct investment flows. For example, the total U.S. direct investment abroad was only $7.2 billion in 1946, but it grew rapidly after the 1950s and reached $54 billion in 1966. Direct investment leveled off in the 1970s and has gained new momentum since the 1980s. The recent growth is further characterized by the uprising of multinational enterprises headquartered in Japan and Western European countries. This international expansion of the firm based on direct investment has been extensively studied, not only because of its importance in terms of size, but also because it represents a business organization form that cannot be adequately explained in the classic economic framework. Consequently, a separate avenue of research is developed, with a specific focus on the economic rationality of foreign direct investment and the multinational enterprise.

While the earlier literature did not explicitly distinguish between international portfolio investment and direct investment, it justifies the cross-border capital movement mainly by interest rate differentials. According to Olin (1933), countries have different factor endowment ratios of labor and capital, and this results in different rates of return for capital. This stimulates the movement of capital from countries of low interest rates to those of high interest rates, as a result of investors' efforts to seek higher rates of investment return. The approach is further extended by MacDougall (1960) and Kemp (1964), who argued that varied capital availability among countries, because of the law of diminishing returns, would lead to different marginal productivity and rates of return for capital across countries. This will spur the movement of capital from the country with a lower rate of return to that with a higher return, and this movement will eventually lead to equalization of the cost of capital worldwide. Although the interest rate differential approach can provide a justification for portfolio investment, it is insufficient to explain foreign direct investment. First, since investors can take advantage of interest rate differentials simply by investing in foreign stock and bond markets, why should they seek direct ownership of operating assets overseas? Second, while U.S., European, and Japanese multinationals actively invest in each other's markets, how can the theory explain this cross investment? Finally, what is the explanation for the pattern of direct investment flows, which predominantly concentrate in a few sectors, such as electronics, chemicals, and food industries?

These critical issues were first addressed by Stephen Hymer in his seminal dissertation completed in 1960 but published posthumously in 1976.

The explanation starts with a clear distinction between international portfolio investment and foreign direct investment. The portfolio investment, through purchase of bonds and stocks, is undertaken mainly to seek gains from international interest differentials, capital appreciation, and diversification of market risk. On the other hand, foreign direct investment is motivated by an entirely different purpose. A firm undertakes direct investment to maintain control over business operations abroad. Here ownership control is the essential issue. The motive can be better understood only when imperfections in the market are recognized. More specifically, foreign direct investment is a strategic response of the firm to the presence of market imperfections and is an instrument used to overcome these imperfections. Various market imperfections identified by Kindleberger (1969) include (1) the imperfections in the goods market associated with product differentiation, special marketing skills, and collusion in pricing; (2) the imperfections in the factor market due to the existence of the patent-protected technology and proprietary technological know-how, and different accesses to capital, management and engineering skills; (3) the existence of internal and external economies of scale; and (4) market distortions created by government policies such as restrictions on imports. As the argument further goes, in a world without these imperfections, FDI would not occur. Instead, various market arrangements, such as trade, licensing, and management contracts, would be developed to organize international exchange.

The Hymer-Kindleberger paradigm presents a research framework that is still followed by today's mainstream literature. In this framework, foreign direct investment is considered an alternative to the market mode for international expansion, and its occurrence is further rationalized on various grounds. See Table 1.1 for a description of foreign direct investment versus various market arrangements for international involvements.

THE CAUSE: STRUCTURAL OR TRANSACTIONAL MARKET IMPERFECTIONS?

Since Hymer's work, an impressive body of literature has emerged. This research, noticeably, has shifted its focus from the original intention to rationalize foreign direct investment to the current attempt to examine the nature of the multinational enterprise. Overall, the MNE has been conceptualized as an economic institution that engages in direct investment and alternative modes of market transactions to exploit foreign opportunities. More specifically, FDI is a substitute for market exchange and is used to replace transactions that otherwise would take place in the market with various imperfections. Furthermore, the literature has identified two major

Table 1.1
Major Forms of MNEs' International Involvements

A. Foreign direct investment takes place when a firm undertakes an investment to acquire ownership control over production organized in a foreign country. The returns for this involvement consist of net profits from business operations and payments from the transfer of intermediate products such as supplies and technological know-how from its foreign affiliates.

B. Market arrangements refer to the arm's length transactions across countries and between firms of separate ownership entities and include various forms like the following:

(1) Export involves the shipment of finished products to foreign buyers.

(2) Turnkey project is an arrangement under which a contractor constructs plant facilities and transfers them to the owner after completion in return for certain payments. It involves the sales of capital goods as well as technological know-how.

(3) Licensing is a legal contract under which the licensor grants the licensee rights to use its intangible property rights for a specified duration in return for some payments. These rights include patents, copyrights, trademarks, and franchises, and also often involve unpatented know-how such as production methods and quality control.

(4) Franchising is a particular form of licensing agreement under which the franchisor provides the franchisee the right to use a trademark or brand name plus technical services, in return for certain payments.

(5) Management contract is an arrangement under which a firm performs certain management functions for another unrelated firm in return for a fee.

(6) Marketing contract is an arrangement under which a firm is assigned the responsibility for marketing products for their producer in return for a fee, generally a certain percentage of sales.

(7) International subcontracting is an arrangement under which a firm contracts a foreign firm to produce components or assemble finished products, supplying inputs and technology related to the production.

C. Joint venture is one form of foreign direct investment which involves several owners who share the resources, operation control, risk, and profits from the investment.

Source: Compiled from UNCTC, *Transnational Corporations and Technology Transfer* (1987).

types of market imperfections—the structural market imperfections and transactional market imperfections.[1] However, when it comes to the question of which one is the major cause of foreign investment, different views still exist, and this difference leads to two separate avenues of scholarly work.

The structural market imperfection refers to certain features of market structure under which perfect competition yields to imperfect competition, ranging from monopolistic competition, to oligopoly, to monopoly. Here, the market structure, including the number of sellers in the market, the size of these firms, the existence of scale economy, and the extent of product differentiation, represents the configuration of the market in which the competing firms interact. According to industrial organization economics, the structural feature of the market has a profound effect on industry performance measured by profitability, growth, and technical progress, and it further determines the productive efficiency of the economy in terms of resources allocation and economic welfare. The distinctive contribution of Joe Bain (1956) lies in his analytical work on entry barriers to the industry. While holding that an industry can maintain sustained higher profitability only if substantial entry barriers exist, he further presented evidence showing the conscious effort of oligopolistic firms to erect barriers against new entry to the industries. Bain's insights provide a conceptual basis for Hymer's study of the multinational enterprise. The analysis begins with the fact that foreign direct investment takes place mainly in highly concentrated industries, and its conclusion is that this investment is a strategic conduct of an oligopolistic firm and is pursued by the firm to remove competition and enhance its market power. Subsequent literature is further produced in the industrial organization framework, including Vernon (1966, 1974, 1979), Caves (1971, 1974), and Knickerbocker (1973). This line of research considers direct investment mainly as a product of highly concentrated domestic market structure and a device pursued by international oligopolies for strategic gains in the highly imperfect market.

On the other hand, the transactional market imperfections stem from obstacles to organize transactions through the market. The transaction cost approach considers the economic coordination in a modern economy constituting a series of transactions. These transactions can be organized either through the market or by the internal organization of the firm. The property of these two types of transaction was extensively explored by Oliver Williamson (1975) in his well-known "Markets and Hierarchies" framework. Economic exchange can be organized between unrelated parties through the market. This results in the market transaction costs due to the existence of market imperfections, which are mainly attributed to the interface of cognitive deficiencies and specific environmental conditions.

Alternatively, to avoid the cost of using the market, the transactions can be conducted within the firm, but then the internal organization cost is incurred. Given different costs associated with the market mode and internal organization, it is the transaction cost minimization that determines which transaction mode is to be used for each transaction; that is, a mode is selected for one specific type of transactions when it is relatively more efficient than others. When the internal organization is less costly, and thus is preferred, for one type of transaction, the failure of the market takes place. Consequently, the internal organization of the firm supersedes the market, and the hierarchical order substitutes for the price mechanism to direct economic activities and resources allocation. The transaction cost economics provides a conceptual framework to explain the operation of the multinational enterprise. In this approach, foreign direct investment is considered as an economic instrument to bypass the international markets with imperfections and internalize transactions within the firm.

The internalization theory, in the analysis of the multinational enterprise, further emphasizes the market failure associated with transactions of proprietary know-how. Technological know-how is a knowledge-based product and includes elements such as engineering expertise, quality control, and management and marketing skills, which are summarized in Figure 1.1. Typically, the ownership of know-how advantage is one major form of a firm's intangible assets that secures the firm a stream of future cash flows. The firm may exploit the know-how internationally by transferring it to a foreign firm by some market arrangements, such as licensing, management contract, or export of goods embodying know-how. A market approach, however, is difficult to carry out because of market imperfections. The market for know-how is highly imperfect mainly due to the existence of an information asymmetry, wherein the buyer has less information than the seller about the know-how product. The market is imperfect further because of the uncertainty associated with the outcome of know-how application, which is influenced by many internal and external factors. As a result, the market can no longer be an efficient means to organize know-how transactions, and the internal organization becomes a more desirable alternative. Therefore, the firm chooses the self-use of know-how, or to internalize it rather than sell the know-how to an unrelated party. Internalization across national boundaries creates the MNE institution, which by undertaking FDI "transfers intermediate products such as knowledge or technology among its units across different nations while still retaining property rights over such assets" (Dunning and Rugman 1985, p. 228).

In summary the industrial organization and internalization theories emphasize two different aspects of market imperfections as a primary explanation for the MNE, generating the "market power" and "internaliza-

Figure 1.1
Elements of Technological Know-How

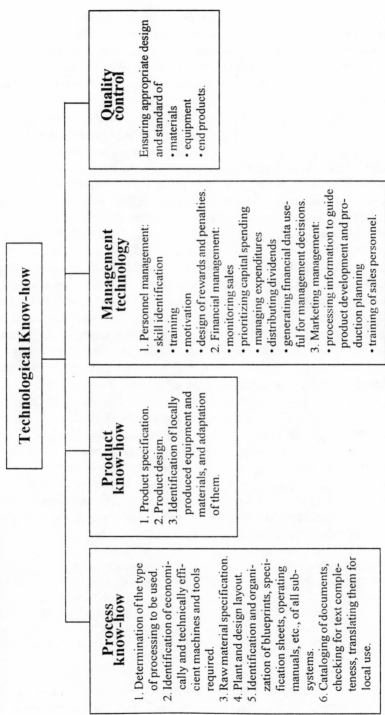

Technological Know-how

Process know-how

1. Determination of the type of processing to be used.
2. Identification of economically and technically efficient machines and tools required.
3. Raw material specification.
4. Plant and design layout.
5. Identification and organization of blueprints, specification sheets, operating manuals, etc., of all subsystems.
6. Cataloging of documents, checking for text completeness, translating them for local use.

Product know-how

1. Product specification.
2. Product design.
3. Identification of locally produced equipment and materials, and adaptation of them.

Management technology

1. Personnel management:
   • skill identification
   • training
   • motivation
   • design of rewards and penalties.
2. Financial management:
   • monitoring sales
   • prioritizing capital spending
   • managing expenditures
   • distributing dividends
   • generating financial data useful for management decisions.
3. Marketing management:
   • processing information to guide product development and production planning
   • training of sales personnel.

Quality control

Ensuring appropriate design and standard of
• materials
• equipment
• end products.

Source: UNCTC, Transnational Corporations in World Development: Trends and Prospects (1988). Used with permission.

tion gain" as two competing hypotheses. Both approaches are based on the established theoretical frameworks and can well explain the rise of the multinational enterprise. The differences lie in their interpretations, which present different implications regarding the efficiency consequences of MNE operations. For that matter, the efficiency consequences can be considered either at the firm level or at the social level. At the firm level, the efficiency of the MNE is rarely questioned. Two theories all recognize this economic institution as a driving force in promoting production efficiency, technological innovation, new product development, and market expansion. Views become less unified, however, when the efficiency is judged from the societal standpoint and on the social consequence of firm-level efficiency. This issue extends the century-old debate on the consequence of corporate domination, "Is there a conflict between 'production for profit' and 'production for use'?" (Drucker 1972, p. 174). Stated alternatively, what is the efficiency consequence of the multinational's operations on the economy as a whole? Does the MNE's pursuit of growth and profit lead to desirable social results in terms of economic growth, output level, economic resources allocation, technological progress, and equity distribution? These are the historical issues that disturb academicians and policymakers alike.

If FDI is motivated mainly by structural market imperfections, it could result in both welfare losses and gains, and the net effect is less clear. As far as Hymer was concerned, "the question of their efficiency [referring to the multinationals] is a question of the efficiency of oligopolistic decision making" (1979, p. 41). Such a view constitutes the basis of the market power hypothesis. This approach focuses on the strategic implication of FDI to the market structure in which the firm operates and believes that the firm's action to take advantage of the imperfections in market structure may lead to a more imperfect market. As a whole the society may stand to lose since the MNE's gains are obtained through further distortions of the market, which results in suboptimal allocation of economic resources and inefficient distribution of products. With much emphasis on structural market imperfections, Hymer's conclusion had to be that

the general presumption of international trade economists in favor of free trade and free factor movements, on the ground of allocative efficiency, does not apply to direct foreign investment because of the anticompetitive effect inherently associated with it . . . [it is] a genuine argument on antimonoply grounds for interfering in international markets. A restriction on direct investment or a policy to break up a multinational corporation may be in some cases the only way of establishing a higher degree of competition in that industry. (1979, p. 46)

With his preoccupation with the market power consideration, Hymer eventually turned into a Marxist economist, and this radical view was further reinforced in his later analytical work on the multinational enterprise (Hymer 1979).

On the other hand, a different conclusion can be generated from "the internalization gain" hypothesis. This approach considers direct investment as an economic solution to transactional market imperfections. These market imperfections are exogenous by nature; that is, they are externally imposed and represent the cost beyond the firm's control (Dunning and Rugman 1985). As a conscious effort to overcome these market imperfections, FDI is undertaken by the firm to create the internal market, which then facilitates international transactions. As a result, some efficiency gains can be generated as a whole, and the multinational's operations should have a positive effect on efficiency at the social level.

In summary, the studies based on the market power and internalization approaches take different stands on the efficiency consequence of the multinational enterprise. This issue can be traced back to a fundamental question: What is "the relationship between the corporation's criterion and yardstick of institutional efficiency, profit, and society's criterion of economic efficiency, maximum production at the lowest cost" (Drucker 1972, p.175)? This is an old issue whose conclusion, however, is beyond theoretical inquiry and has to be determined by empirical research. As Calvet pointed out, it falls to empirical evidence to "shed light on the question of whether MNEs create, extend, and/or perpetuate market imperfections, or whether they are a vehicle for overcoming natural imperfections to the benefits of all parties" (1981, p. 51).

METHODOLOGICAL PITFALLS IN THE RESEARCH

When competing theories exist, empirical research leads the way in providing the key for theoretical differentiation. Given the controversy on the efficiency implication of the MNE, it is not surprising that an impressive volume of empirical literature has been produced in both industrial organization and internalization frameworks. Judged by their empirical accomplishments, these two bodies of literature are at two recognizably different levels. The evidence gathered in the industrial organization studies generally provides conclusive support for the market power hypothesis, suggesting (1) a linkage between the structural market imperfections and FDI, (2) an FDI consequent effect on the market structure of home and host countries, and (3) the tendency for oligopolies to enter specific foreign countries in a close time span. These findings can be interpreted as exclusively supportive of the industrial organization theory. On the other hand, the internalization studies have presented evidence with only weak interpretations. There is no lack of studies allegedly supportive of the theory, but there is a question on the validity of the claim. Virtually none of these studies stand up to scrutiny when the market power and internalization gain are considered as competing hypotheses and if weight is given to prior industrial organization literature. Low empirical content is the major obstacle to the research progress of internalization. Consequently, it is difficult to transform the theory into testable hypotheses and subject it to empirical investigation (for further discussion, see Chapter 3). This led to Kay's criticism a decade ago that "at this level internalization does not satisfy the condition of refutability that is required of a theory" (1983, p. 305).

Kay's dissatisfaction with internalization is a reflection of Karl Popper's ideas on philosophy of science, which are presented in his major writing *The Logic of Scientific Discovery* (1959) and have pervasive influence in the research community. Popper, while believing in the objectivity of knowledge, holds that a theory can never be proved (verified) but only disproved (falsified). A scientific theory should be able to deduct some empirical statements that are falsifiable (i.e., can be refuted by evidence). On the selection of theories, his emphasis is on the corroboration of theories; that is, the extent to which a theory stands up to empirical tests. Lakatos (1970) further recognized that the failure to stand up to a test will not lead to the rejection of a theory. However, an existing theory will be replaced by a new theory if the new theory can explain not only the known existence but also novel facts. Therefore, empiricalness is crucial because "a theory is 'scientific' (or 'acceptable') if it has an 'empirical basis'" (1970, p. 109). The significance of the Lakatosian approach is that it moves the Popperian position from "naive falsificationism" to "sophisticated falsificationism," a modification without compromising Popper's emphasis on the falsifiability of the theory.[2]

The impact of Popper's thought is exemplified by the dominance of positivism in economic research, which is popularized by Milton Friedman's well-known essay "The Methodology of Positive Economics" published in 1953. The positive economics, with a major focus on "what is," is distinguished from the normative theory, whose concern is on "what ought to be" (Keynes 1890). A positive proposition is a statement such as "one firm's entry to a foreign country will trigger the similar action of another firm," which can be confronted by evidence. On the other hand, a normative (prescriptive) statement such as "A firm should invest in different currency zones to diversify foreign exchange risk" cannot be refuted. This proposition, as far as a positivist economist is concerned, is meaningless because it is irrefutable. Positivism, while avoiding value judgment and prescriptive theories, focuses on explanation and prediction. Specifically, explanation means to provide justification for the observed phenomenon, and prediction concerns the unobserved event. The prediction can be a forecast of the future, but can also be an identification of existing but undiscovered relations or phenomena.

The theory on foreign direct investment, with its major purpose to provide explanation, has a strong positivist tradition. The dominance of positivism is further exhibited by the general format of academic publication—first it presents a theoretical framework, which is followed by a sort of empirical evidence, which then is elaborated in the context of the theory. In the positivist research environment, we should have expected to see the prevalence of industrial organization over internalization, given their respective empirical accomplishments. Therefore, it is rather surprising, or even ironic, to see the overwhelming shift of emphasis from structural market to transactional market imperfections in current research. A two-decade search has converged on internalization with a basis on transaction cost economics. The popularization of internalization is further reflected by the sheer volume of publication. This outcome is at odds with the empirical stagnation of internalization and is contradictory to Popper's projection that "the degree of their testability is of significance for the selection of theories" (1959, p. 112). It only confirms McCloskey's position that it is rhetoric—"the aptness of economic metaphors, the relevance of historical precedents, the persuasiveness of introspections, the power of authority, the charm of symmetry, the claims of morality" (1983, p. 482)—that conditions economists' choices.

The popularity of internalization seems to be more in keeping with Kuhn's view on the theorization process. While denying the objective nature of knowledge, Kuhn suggested that the selection of the theory should be psychological or sociological:

It must, that is, be a description of a value system, an ideology, together with an analysis of the institution through which that system is transmitted and enforced. Knowing what scientists value, we may hope to understand what problems they will undertake and what choices they will make in particular circumstances of conflict. (1970, p. 21)

An extension of this view in a radical direction is offered by Habermas (1972) in his critique of social science research. He argued that facts can be reconstructed to fit the theory and the world is articulated through language, which is conditioned by researchers' values and beliefs.

Clearly, the sociological approach considers that social context is an important factor in influencing the evolution of FDI theories. For that matter, we may take a look at the global sociopolitical environment of the multinational enterprise. The environment has experienced remarkable transformation in the last two decades. Today, all nation-states must confront challenges stemming from international competition, technological advances and economic growth. In the current world setting, an increasing recognition of a global horizon has replaced the old concern with the "bigness" of business, and policymakers are more motivated by economic considerations than by political imperatives. Along with these changes, there is a renewed attitude toward multinational enterprises, which now are portrayed as "Everybody's Favourite Monsters."[3] Although the old resentment and fear still exist, they are surmounted by overriding economic considerations. Consequently, since the 1970s there has been a significant drop in expropriation of foreign corporate assets. Foreign direct investment has been generally accepted as a means to access capital, technology, and the world market. Even countries such as former Soviet Union states, China, and Vietnam, which were hostile to the capitalist export of capital, eagerly encourage foreign investment inflows. In the current world atmosphere, the internalization theory apparently has a public appeal because it can be used conveniently to interpret the multinational as an agent promoting social efficiency and economic gains on a global scale.

Undoubtedly, the sociological approach can explain the popularization of internalization. This explanation, however, would be uncomfortable, even disturbing, for economists because it implies that the researcher is, consciously or unconsciously, a captive of conventional wisdom and produces theories only to support the prevailing social perception and political objectives. Therefore, it is not surprising that the internalization theorist sees the significance of improving the empirical basis of internalization. Buckley (1988), after an overall assessment of the theory, conceded that the internalization framework is irrefutable at a general level. While calling it "an urgent task" to overcome the empirical obstacle, he foresaw that some special theories might be developed for an indirect test of the internalization theory.

That suggestion may show the direction to follow in overcoming the empirical stagnation of internalization because it also conforms to the methodology of scientific research programs (MSRPs) described by Lakatos (1970). According to Lakatos, the growth of science is characterized by the development of successive scientific research programs. The scientific research programs consist of the negative heuristic and the positive heuristic. The negative heuristic is the program's "hard core," which is irrefutable. For example, the hard core of internalization theory is the doctrine of transaction cost economization—the firm chooses among alternative transaction modes to minimize transaction costs—and it cannot be empirically tested. The MSRP also contains the positive heuristic of "auxiliary hypotheses," which are refutable and form a protective belt around the hard core. The progress of MSRP is a history which shows how the researcher adheres to the hard core by presenting ad hoc modification, theoretical extension, and empirical evidence. In this course, a research program is considered progressive problemshifts when its development leads to consistent enhancement of empirical content, and it is considered degenerating problemshifts when it results in diminishing empirical content. The Lakatosian approach has a prescriptive power in guiding successful research progress, suggesting that the researcher should avoid the path of negative heuristic and pursue the path of positive heuristic. The implication to the current internalization research is that it should seek progress through expansion of a positive heuristic, that is, to enhance its empirical content by deriving some auxiliary theories with empirical implications. Evidently Buckley (1988) follows this route when he suggests the development of a special theory as a way to advance the empirical research of internalization.

THE SIGNALING EFFECT OF FOREIGN DIRECT INVESTMENT

The preceding discussion of the literature on foreign direct investment is rather lengthy but is necessary for understanding the issues to be addressed here. This book will construct the signaling framework of foreign direct investment based on a synthesis of internalization and signaling literature. The recognition of the FDI signaling effect allows us to elaborate on the transactional market consequences of direct investment, with which some important empirical implications are derived and thus the internalization hypothesis can be tested indirectly. Therefore, the FDI signaling framework enhances the empirical content of internalization and leads to "progressive problemshifts." This reverses the trend of degenerating research due to the increasing irrefutability of the current literature. In short, this research is developed in a direction suggested by Buckley and thus conforming to Lakatos's prescription of progressive research.

The internalization theory centers on transactional market imperfections, particularly the imperfections associated with transactions of know-how. It has been recognized that when the market presents asymmetric information, and when the buyer is less informed than the seller, the market cannot correctly evaluate know-how products. This problem is suggested as a major cause for FDI internalization and the firm's preference for self-use of know-how. We extend the analysis by recognizing the existence of market mechanisms to overcome market imperfections. Notice that the availability of the internalization solution has not replaced the market completely. In fact, the market has experienced substantial growth, and today the MNE is more likely to use the market arrangements for international involvements (UNCTC 1988). Although the firm's choice between the market and the internal organization can be explained by the transaction cost economics, questions still can be raised: How do transactions proceed in the market with known imperfections? Are there any means available in the market to cope with this problem? It is also worthwhile to consider possible institutional mechanisms developed by the firm to attenuate the named market imperfections.

In this book, these issues are explored in the context of the signaling theory. A market signal is defined as an action adopted by the firm which, by design or unintentionally, conveys information to less informed market participants and changes their beliefs or perceptions (Spence 1974). Suppose there are two games, one with the chance and dollar amount to win directly tied to a participant's intelligence level and the other purely determined by luck. Assume that there are two levels of human intelligence, high and low, which are unobservable, but individuals all know their own intelligence levels. Further assume that the rules of two games are understood by all participants and that each of them has the freedom to choose the game to play. Since all participants seek to maximize their own monetary gains, the free choice will lead to self-selection—ones with high intelligence are likely to participate in the former game, and ones with low intelligence in the latter game. Consequently, the action of choice becomes a signal because it reveals the intelligence levels, the unobservable feature of individuals.

Based on this example, the basic idea of signaling is quite simple. When a firm has certain attributes unknown to the public (in the example, an individual's intelligence) but makes a choice of action that is observable (the chosen game), if this choice is based on the state of its hidden attributes and is made to serve self-interest (maximize the person's own gains), then the observed action of choice will reveal the firm's unobservable attributes to the public (unobservable intelligence). In other words, this action conveys information across the market and alters the perception of less informed market participants. The important implication is that signaling attenuates the asymmetric structure of information in the market. As Spence (1973) suggested, market signaling should develop in the market with asymmetric information about the product quality because (1) the firm of good quality has a strong incentive to correct the initial information asymmetry and differentiate its products, and (2) the buyer will seek to screen firms in the market by taking cues from the firm behavior.

The insights of signaling literature can be readily applicable to research on the multinational enterprise. A similar kind of perceptual impact may result from the firm's action to undertake direct investment, even if it is not the firm's original intention. The FDI signaling proposition can be logically derived from the internalization theory, only with a recognition of interactions between the firm and other market participants. If the existing theory is correct that FDI internalization is motivated by information imperfection in the market, this action would then affect the perception of these less informed outsiders. As we know, when information is not completely available, outsiders will make certain inferences about the firm based on the observed behavior of the firm. When a firm chooses to use FDI internalization as a means to exploit its know-how advantages, this action further reflects its management belief that the know-how possessions are more valuable than average or than what is perceived by the market. While management's decision is based on certain inside information (the information unknown to the market), its decision revealed in its action has revealed this information to the public. In other words, the FDI action has information content. Upon seeing the firm's investment action, outsiders will conclude, correctly, that the firm has a know-how-based intangible asset more valuable than what is perceived by the market. Therefore, the firm's FDI action may constitute a signal which affects the market perception.

The FDI signaling proposition further provides implications to interrelationships between the firm and other market participants, such as know-how buyers, consumers, and investors. Ostensibly, if a firm's direct investment posture alters the perception of less informed outsiders, this posture should also have a consequent effect on their behavior. Such perceptual and behavioral consequences are likely to be recognized by the firm, even before it takes the FDI action. As such, the firm may undertake FDI with an anticipation of its effect on outsiders. In other words, the firm may adjust its FDI posture to seek maximum gains from the expected perceptual effects. Therefore, there are actions and reactions among market participants, and they are all interrelated in an interactive setting. Based on the FDI signaling theory, several important implications can be presented. First, the firm's FDI posture may further affect its operations in the external market, since it signals the firm's know-how capability. Second, the MNE should be a global optimizer. With the existence of the signaling effect, a firm makes a decision on FDI based not only on the expected profits from foreign operations but also on the market gains associated with perceptual effects. Then it would adopt an integrated approach to its foreign expansion, carefully choosing between foreign production and various market modes for each overseas expansion, with the purpose of maximizing its total profits from various foreign involvements.[4]

THE RELEVANCE OF FDI SIGNALING RESEARCH

The concept of FDI signaling was sporadically mentioned in the literature. Casson (1987), in his rationalization of FDI, postulated that a firm's establishment of foreign production signals its commitment to the market of the host country. A similar idea can be found in the literature even before that. For instance, Aharoni quoted a foreign investor: "It is also a chain reaction. We make [production x] in India. People see our name, they know us, so they buy our [products y and z] that are imported from the United States" (1966, p. 71). However, the FDI signaling effect has never been systematically examined in the context of theories of foreign direct investment. If so, why should we now engage in such a study, particularly when there is a body of literature that thoroughly examines the FDI issue and provides sound justification? In other words, what is the additional gain from recognizing the FDI signaling effect? There are several reasons. First, the FDI signaling theory explains certain aspects of MNE behavior and patterns of its foreign involvement that cannot be justified by the existing theory. Second, the research in FDI signaling further develops a conceptual link between the MNE's FDI internalization and market transactions, which is not clear in the existing theoretical framework. Finally, the FDI signaling research provides a building block for empirical internalization. By recognizing the FDI signaling effect, we may develop a framework to test the internalization theory indirectly and thus correct the empirical deficiency of the theory.

There are many examples which show the firms' apparent eagerness not only to expand overseas but also to publicize the multinational nature of its business. The author had the experience of being a consultant for Taiwan's network marketing company, which is a distributor of a wide range of health and cosmetic products. The company has a laboratory in Los Angeles, California, which lacks operational efficiency mainly because of its small scale and low level of technical content. Although this laboratory has a cost of production often higher than that of procuring similar goods in the market, this company still maintains this operation on its existing scale and as a supplier of a few products. This existence, however, allows the company to brag of the international nature of its business, which is always emphasized in the company's brochures and catalogues with the cover pages showing the pictures of its foreign establishment. Essentially, the company's practice is to pay a price to preserve its membership in the international business club.

Another example is the Capital Steel and Iron Complex (CSIC) in Beijing, China, one of China's largest state-owned enterprises and a high-profile showcase in the country's economic reform. In 1988 the company took a strategic action, paying $6 million to acquire a 70% share of Mester International Co., an engineering firm in Pittsburgh, Pennsylvania that specialized in the design of steel-mill equipment. This foreign acquisition has produced only losses. Again, in 1993, CSIC spent $120 million to purchase a state-owned iron mine in Peru, and that deal was an even bigger flop. Top management was reprimanded for these imprudent investment decisions. The CSIC's experiences may have revealed its lack of ability to play the global market. However, a relevant question is, What motivated the company to take such aggressive actions for foreign expansion? According to a former Chinese expatriate to Mester, these acquisitions were fueled mainly by top management's ambition to become China's first multinational enterprise. This view is supported by the fact that CSIC's foreign acquisitions received widespread media coverage in China. However, these highly publicized actions later turned out to be costly experiences for the company.

While these oriental stories suggest that foreign direct investment results from the firm's desire to acquire the MNE reputation, it could also be argued that they are exceptional cases. However, we can further find a similar behavior pattern among Western firms. A case in point is shown in Example 1.1, which details the public accounting profession's entry in China. It shows that the major Western accounting firms established an early presence in China mainly to seek publicity gains rather than direct economic benefits.

Although these incidents do not represent the mainstream foreign investment, they do reflect the firm's tendency to emphasize its multinational status as a way of market promotion. This behavior cannot be adequately explained by the existing FDI theories, whose rationalization is based mainly on the argument that the investment is economically a more profitable means to exploit foreign opportunities. This behavior, however, can be well justified in the FDI signaling framework. The major argument of this book is that the firm, while acknowledging the FDI signaling effect, would pursue an FDI strategy not only for investment profits but also to capitalize on the cognitive effect to maximize its overall gains from foreign operations.

The FDI signaling concept further sheds light on corporate behavior in voluntary disclosure of foreign operations, as discussed in Example 1.2. The Financial Accounting Standard Board (FASB) rule requires American corporations to provide separate disclosure for their foreign operations when this involvement reaches a certain level. However, many U.S. public corporations adopt voluntary foreign disclosure, that is, report the foreign operation results even if this involvement is below the required disclosure level. The accounting literature suggests that voluntary disclosure have information content, which is conveyed either by the disclosure (e.g., the foreign earnings reported) or by the act to choose such a disclosure (i.e., the firm's willingness to disclose may say something). However, we may exclude the former type as a cause because, if the foreign information disclosed is significant, its disclosure would be compulsory. Thus it should

Example 1.1   Big Accounting Firms Entered China for Publicity Gains

The public accounting profession is one of the most multinationalized industries, with the "Big Six" accounting firms, Arthur Andersen, Coopers & Lybrand, Deloitte & Touche, Ernst & Young, KPMG Peat Marwick, and Price Waterhouse all operating under a global network partnership and having business in up to over a hundred countries. In recent years, these firms have established offices in major Chinese cities such as Beijing and Shanghai. This is not surprising since China now is a major host country of foreign direct investment. According to the World Bank report, China attracted $26 billion foreign investment in 1993, which makes it the second largest recipient of foreign capital, second only to the United States. When those major multinationals go to China, their auditors should follow suit.

However, a closer look suggests that the "following customers" argument may not be a complete explanation for public accounting's earlier expansion to China. This entrance started around the late 1970s, shortly after China adopted the economic reform and open-door policy, but long before it attracted any major foreign investment. To obtain official approval for their entries, these accounting firms competed with each other in volunteering services to the Chinese government, including technical consulting, management seminars, and on-the-job training for Chinese nationals. This approach was costly but did not open up the prospect for profits since China's economy was still under state ownership and tight central control. Then it must be for the long-term potential of China's market, as the argument often goes. However, why couldn't these accounting firms wait until this potential materializes? The wait-and-see strategy would make sense particularly because the nature of public accounting, which suggests that their business come up there most likely as a result of their multinational clients' expansion to that market.

While these accounting firms' involvement in China did not generate the immediate economic gains, it brought them noticeable publicity gains. During that time, one of these firms, Touche Ross, brought the author to its Toronto office to participate in the on-the-job training program. His role there, however, was social rather than accounting related. The firm sought to capitalize on the presence of their Chinese trainees by introducing them to the public circle and press, which resulted in coverage in *The Global Mail* (the largest business newspaper in Canada) and the appearance on *Everybody's Business* on The Global Channel and on the *Betty Kennedy Show* on the CFRB radio station. The similar public exposure was also arranged for the Chinese trainees who went to other accounting firms. Is this a skillfully orchestrated maneuver to promote the firms' image, by publicizing their expansion to a new territory which was large but still mysterious to the public?

In conclusion, does this case suggest that some firms undertake foreign investment for reasons other than direct operating profits? If so, how should this be related to the existing theory of foreign direct investment?

be the latter type, which suggests that the firm seek to tell the market something by self-imposed foreign disclosure. Then the next question is, What kind of information does the firm intend to convey? While this corporate behavior cannot be satisfactorily explained by current FDI literature, it can be better understood when the FDI signaling effect is recognized. If the FDI has a signaling effect, then voluntary foreign disclosure may be an act that further conveys information about the value of intangible assets to the market.

Another implication of the FDI signaling concept is that the MNE's foreign investment, like advertising and other kinds of market promotion activities, may have a positive effect on the firm's image and on its brand recognition. This effect can be shown by the consequence of one multinational's expansion in China. This country, with its rapid economic growth and huge population, has emerged as a potential market for many consumer goods. Its beer consumption market, for instance, has grown into the second largest, and soon will be the largest, in the world. The foreign MNE with the strongest market position there unquestionably is Pabst Brewing Co., because Lan Dai (Chinese words meaning Blue Ribbon) is a household name in China now. Lan Dai has achieved this kind of popularity only because the company was the first one to set up a joint venture to serve the beer market in China and thus easily build up consumer awareness of its products. Considering the potential of that market, this brand recognition carries a significant premium. Although this example shows the relationship between the MNE's foreign investment and its foreign subsidiary sales (which can be explained by the internalization theory), by recognizing the perceptual effect of FDI, we further conjecture that the firm's FDI expansion promotes its overseas market position and thus its market transactions such as direct exports.

Intuitively, a complementary relationship is suggested for the MNE's internalization and externalization. This implication has significance in the interpretation of today's economic globalization. The MNE has been seen as an economic institution relentlessly expanding the foreign production scale. While the internalization theory suggests that this investment be a solution to transactional market imperfections and result in efficiency gains, the FDI signaling theory further argues that this should not be a cause for the fear of market destruction. That is because FDI expansion will further promote transactions in the market. This conjecture is consistent with evidence, which suggests that the FDI expansion has been achieved at no expense of international market activities. In the last two decades, MNEs have become particularly active in foreign involvements through various forms of market arrangements. In 1993, for example, U.S. multinationals' exports to unaffiliated foreigners reached $139 billion, which represents

Example 1.2   Does Voluntary Foreign Disclosure Convey Information to the Market?

Although the United States still represents the world's most important capital market, not many leading foreign multinationals choose to list on U.S. stock exchanges. The main reason is the strict financial disclosure requirements adopted by the U.S. Securities and Exchange Commission (SEC), which are considered excessive and revealing of too much proprietary information. Therefore, when Daimler-Benz decided to be the first German firm to be listed on the New York Stock Exchange in 1993, it surprised the German business community. After the firm represented its financial statements in conformance with U.S. Generally Accepted Accounting Principles (GAAP), its earnings of $97 million turned out to be a loss of $548 million.

Consequently, it is generally believed that corporations resist public pressure for additional disclosure and report information only when required by regulation. This attitude, however, does not reflect the practice of foreign operations disclosure. The rule for this disclosure is established by the Financial Accounting Standard Board in Statement of Financial Accounting Standards (SFAS) No. 14, *Financial Reporting for Segments of a Business Enterprise*. The provision requires a firm to provide a foreign segment report if its identifiable foreign assets and/or foreign sales represent 10% or more of the consolidated assets and sales. The rationale underlying the mandatory disclosure is that when a firm's foreign operation is significant enough to affect its overall prospect of earnings and risk, investors should be informed. The 10% threshold reflects the accounting concept of *materiality,* which suggests that accounting disclosure should be limited only to the information that matters in decision making. In other words, the foreign operation representing a segment less than 10% of total may not be considered *material*.

In practice, however, foreign disclosure often goes to an extent well beyond what is required by the rule. Many U.S. corporations adopt voluntary foreign disclosure, reporting their foreign segments even if this is not required. For example, the author retrieved from the Value Line database all U.S. firms that reported foreign operations in the 1977–83 period. Of 825 firms reporting foreign operations, 223 have both foreign assets and sales less than 10% of consolidated assets and sales. Some companies even have the reported foreign segments representing less than 1% of the total.

An interesting question can be raised: What is the motivation for voluntary foreign disclosure? Because the firm volunteers the disclosure, it must seek to tell the market something. Furthermore, while management has the incentive to reveal it, this something must be positive news. However, it is unlikely to foreign performance per se. That is because if that information is *material* (i.e., it carries a weight significant enough to alter the investor's perception), the disclosure would be mandatory. Then, what information? The alternative explanation is that the act of voluntary disclosure has information content. This is consistent to the FDI signaling proposition, which suggests that the FDI action convey information about the firm's intangible assets.

56% of their total exports. Their receipts of royalties and licensing fees from unaffiliated foreign firms topped $4.6 billion, which represents 24% of their total receipts in this category (Figure B.1). The evidence also shows that MNEs have modified their traditional approach to use FDI as the major means of know-how transfer. A hybrid of external and internal market arrangements such as minority ownership and joint ventures is increasingly used as a mode for foreign entry (Table B.1).

All these facts are consistent with the FDI signaling framework. In its context, the MNE's internalization and externalization all are integral parts of a globalization process. They are not only economic choices but also mutually supportive and lead to promoting each other's positions, which leads to a higher level of internationalization of the firm. Recognition of FDI signaling extends the internalization theory and provides a more comprehensive perspective on the implications of foreign direct investment.[5]

A significant contribution of FDI signaling research is the enhancement of the internalization theory's empirical content. The validity of that school has been challenged because of its weak empirical basis. One way to overcome the empirical difficulty is to develop some special theories and subject internalization to an indirect test. This objective can be accomplished by research in the FDI signaling framework. The signaling effect can be empirically measured, for example, by examining the market reactions (e.g., the stock price adjustment) to the proposed signaling action. In this way, the hypothesized information content of FDI signaling is falsifiable. However, the FDI signaling proposition is further derived from, and critically depends on, the validity of the internalization hypothesis. Therefore, the FDI signaling test is constructed as a joint test of the FDI signaling hypothesis and internalization gain hypothesis. A rejection of FDI signaling may not necessarily be a rejection of internalization, but an acceptance of FDI signaling should lead to the acceptance of internalization. As such, the development of the FDI signaling concept provides an alternative approach to indirectly testing the internalization theory. As shown in Chapter 6 and Chapter 7, the evidence is interpreted in the internalization framework.

A major point can be made before the close of this chapter. The FDI signaling theory develops its explanatory power not by rejecting the existing theory or formulating a new theory. Rather it is an extension of internalization and integrates well with the existing framework. In other words, while the power of the existing theory remains intact, the FDI signaling theory provides additional explanations and substantially advances our understanding of many issues related to the MNE and its foreign investments. That is a major strength of this research.

NOTES

1. For example, see the major review on the accomplishments and research frameworks provided by Dunning and Rugman (1985), Teece (1985), and Horaguchi and Toyne (1990).

2. In reality, with the complexity of this world, no theory can provide a perfect explanation and there are always unexplained anomalies. Competing theories always exist, and scientific growth is the choice made among imperfect theories. Consequently, the Popperian approach is exposed to major criticism by Kuhn (1962), who argues that if every theory is thrown out once it is falsified, then no theory will be left. The methodology of scientific research programs (MSRPs) developed by Lakatos, on the other hand, represents a compromise between Popper's ahistorical position and Kuhn's sociological relativism, but is "a compromise which stays within the Popperian camp" (Blaug 1976, p. 155).

3. The term is used as a title for a special survey on multinational enterprises conducted by the British magazine *The Economist* (March 27, 1993 issue).

4. In the transaction cost paradigm, the MNE is assumed to minimize its total transaction costs. However, as Grosse (1985) and Tang and Yu (1990) suggested, the approaches of profit maximization and transaction cost minimization do not lead to the same outcome unless alternative transaction modes generate the same streams of revenues.

5. The internalization theory recognizes mainly the substitution effect of FDI because this investment leads to the internalization of transactions that otherwise would take place in the external market. Such an inference leads to the once-popular proposition that the MNE's increasingly internal transfer of know-how may lead to greater "dis-internalization" of international transactions (Contractor and Safafi-nejad 1981). This prediction, however, has never come to pass in practice.

2

Multinational and Foreign Investment: Issues and Previous Theories

Traditionally the nation-state is a major subset of the human world. The nation-state groups people of similar language, history and cultural heritage and fosters the internal bond by promoting uniform sociopolitical institutions, economic systems, and infrastructures. Therefore, it is natural to look at the national boundary as the major demarcation for a productive economy. The national firm operates in the nation-state, from product development, supplies procurement, and production coordination to marketing and distribution of finished products. However, since the relative proportion of factor endowments differs across countries, each nation has an absolute advantage and a comparative advantage in certain types of production. This gives rises to economic gains through national specialization. In a perfectly competitive market, with the assumption that goods are mobile and production factors immobile, international exchange will take place—each nation concentrates on the production in which it has the advantage and acquires through trade the goods that it does not produce. Free trade, through interaction of competitive market forces, will yield the best allocation of economic resources. International specialization and exchange will benefit peoples of all nations alike. This is the economic scenario described by Adam Smith and David Ricardo over 200 hundred years ago.

Since then, the world has experienced enormous transformation as a consequence of technological progress, economic growth, and development of international political and economic institutions. Despite these changes, the basic framework presented by the classic economists remains valid. Some old concepts may be obsolete. For example, the rigid assumption of factor immobility needs to be relaxed to reflect the transferrable nature of

Table 2.1

U.S. Merchandise Trade and the Trade Associated with Nonbank U.S. Multinational Enterprises

(Billion dollars, except where noted)

	1983	1984	1985	1986	1987	1988	1989	1990	1991	1992	1993
(1) MNE Exports	154	169	171	171	184	215	236	241	258	266	270
(2) Total. Exports	202	219	216	223	250	320	364	393	422	448	465
MNE/Total (%)	(76)	(77)	(79)	(77)	(74)	(67)	(65)	(61)	(61)	(59)	(58)
(3) MNE Imports	125	146	155	147	167	181	201	213	213	220	231
(4) Total Imports	269	332	338	368	410	447	474	500	488	533	581
MNE/Total (%)	(46)	(44)	(46)	(40)	(41)	(40)	(42)	(43)	(44)	(41)	(40)
(5) Net of MNE trade = (1) − (3)	29	23	16	24	17	34	35	28	45	46	39
(6) U.S. trade position = (2) − (4)	−67	−113	−122	−145	−160	−127	−110	−107	−66	−85	−116

Source: U.S. Department of Commerce, Bureau of Economic Analysis, *Current Survey of Business*, various issues.

Note: The figures in the parentheses are the MNE's trade as a percentage of total U.S. trade.

some production factors. One such factor is technology. A national firm may transfer its technology to another firm in a foreign country by some market arrangements such as licensing, management contracts, and turnkey projects. In this scenario trade still can be established as a viable choice in achieving international specialization and allocative efficiency of world economies. The importance of trade is further confirmed by international trade statistics. In the past twenty-five years, the growth of trade has been twice as large as the growth of world output, and world merchandise trade amounted to $4.06 trillion in 1994. This indicates that additional efficiency gains have been obtained by progressive international specialization, and the global economic prosperity depends on the growth of trade.

Figure 2.1
U.S. MNEs' Intrafirm and Direct Exports

Billion Dollars

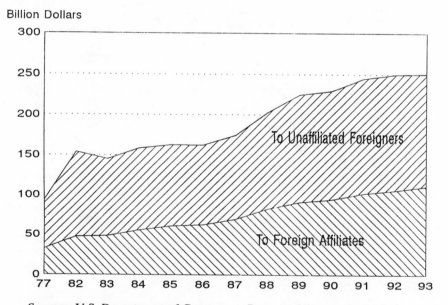

Sources: U.S. Department of Commerce, Bureau of Economic Analysis, *U.S. Direct Investment Abroad,* various issues.

This is the traditional approach with which to present the picture of trade statistics. This approach, however, has obscured the important role of multinationals in international trade. The significance the MNE in the U.S. trade is reflected by the trade data in Table 2.1. As it shows, the MNE's exports constitute well over 50% of U.S. total exports, and its imports over 40% of total imports, and in net it earns trade surpluses consistently for the United States. Thus, contradictory to some common beliefs, the MNE as a group positively contributes to the balance of payments during the period when this country has a deteriorating trade position. Figure 2.1 further shows that for the trade conducted by U.S. multinationals, a significant amount (about 40-50%) takes place within the firm between parent companies and their foreign affiliates. The salient feature of intrafirm trade is that transactions organized under uniform ownership have superseded arm's length transactions. This uniform ownership results from the firms' expansion of foreign direct investment. The relative position of U.S. direct investment and trade is further reported in Figure 2.2, which shows that in the last fifteen years direct investment led trade in promoting the internationalization of the U.S. economy. In short, the review of global economic factors concludes that the MNE and foreign direct investment cannot help but have precedence over trade.

Figure 2.2
U.S. Exports and Direct Investment Position

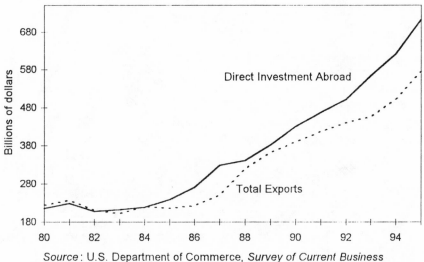

Source: U.S. Department of Commerce, *Survey of Current Business*

This MNE institution—in searching for expansion opportunities—knows no national boundaries and is halted by no geographic constraints. Seagram Company, a Canadian beverage producer, generates 98% of its total sales from overseas operations. The computer giant IBM has 40% of its world employment located overseas, with IBM Japan hiring more than 18,000 local employees. McDonald's Company, the world's largest fast-food chain, sells hamburgers in 14,000 restaurants in seventy countries around the globe. Bayer Ag, the German pharmaceutical giant, has its stocks listed simultaneously on the Frankfurt, New York and London stock exchanges. Ford Motor Company boasts of itself as a producer of a global car, with the design and major components and parts completed in different regions of the world and the final product assembled in still another country. These giant corporations all have displayed a common attribute: The national identity is no longer a crucial measure with which to portray a picture of the firm's business.

KEY ISSUES ADDRESSED IN THE RESEARCH

The operation of the multinational enterprise not only becomes a major alternative to the traditional economic model of trade, but also challenges classical economic thinking. It represents a production mode strikingly different from the one that organizes international economic activity through market coordination. The essential function of direct investment is to bring business units of different nationalities under common ownership control, which allows the firm to substitute internal organization for the market and thus to direct economic coordination and resources allocation across countries. Through this investment, the MNE establishes a centrally directed organizational structure, suppressing the price mechanism with the administrative order and pursuing global maximization rather than separate optimization of individual units scattered across countries.

Upon the arrival of the MNE institution, therefore, we can readily identify two major organizational structures with which to coordinate the international division of labor—the first one is the specialization achieved by national firms, which is coordinated by the markets, and the second one is the specialization achieved by the multinational firm, which is coordinated by the corporate hierarchy (Hymer 1979). However, it has also been recognized that there is a drawback in operating under the second economic mode. The multinational enterprise has disadvantages in competing with a native firm in a foreign country. First, it is more costly for international communication and for coordination and control of operations at a distance (Hirsch 1976). Second, the MNE is less familiar with the local conditions in terms of culture, language, and customs and has less understanding of local markets. Third, the firm may have more risk exposure, including foreign exchange risk, which affects the firm's value when it has assets and cash flows denominated in different currencies, and political risk, which is less a concern in a domestic setting because it affects all national firms alike. Finally, the MNE is likely to face host government policies that discriminate against foreign firms. Consequently, the MNE should incur additional operating costs in the foreign country.

Despite these operational disadvantages, the multinational enterprise has emerged as a predominant economic institution for conducting international business. As in Charles Darwin's theory of species survival, when there are competing modes for organizing economic activity, the most efficient organizational structure will prevail. In other words, the existence justifies itself, and the survival and upsurge of the MNE is self-evident of its institutional efficiency in pursuing international economic coordination (of course, this is the efficiency at the firm's level and measured by its profitability; it may not be interpreted in the society context). Consequently, the explanation for foreign direct investment must go beyond the classical economic framework.

The search for this explanation has led to the development of new theoretical paradigms. Despite their claims, not all of these works can be considered as the theory of foreign direct investment. To be qualified as such a theory, the research should establish its framework based on the essential features of this foreign involvement. First, it should consider the operational aspect of foreign direct investment, which mainly is international production (or direct foreign operation) rather than instrumentation of financial devices. Second, it should recognize the investment as a substitute for international trade, resulting from a firm's conscious choice of internal organization as the replacement of market transactions. Third, it should demonstrate why the firm's hierarchial control can be more efficient than the market in coordination of international economic activities, even with the recognized additional cost associated with foreign production. In short, a true theory of foreign direct investment must aim at these critical issues. Indeed, it is by addressing these issues that the contemporary research has distinguished itself from the classical paradigm, which is on the premise of perfect competition assumption and thus is inadequate in justifying the MNE institution and its foreign investment.

This clarification allows us to exclude several schools as candidates for the theory of foreign direct investment. The international diversification approach, for example, may not be the theoretical justification for foreign direct investment. Evidence shows that fluctuations in corporate earnings and sales are reduced for U.S. firms involved in foreign operations (Cohen 1972, Rugman 1976). Based on a review of the performance of international goods and capital markets, Rugman (1979) concluded that the investment in stocks of domestic MNEs can be a surrogate for international diversification. Thus risk reduction adds an additional economic incentive for direct investment. It, however, cannot be the ultimate motive. For that purpose, the purchase of stocks in foreign capital markets can be a more effective approach (Jacquillat and Solnik 1978), which is a viable means with popularization of various international mutual funds in recent years.

A similar comment can be made about Aliber's work (1970, 1983). Aliber suggested that exchange rates be established in the market in such a way that weak currencies carry a risk premium, reflecting the risk-averse nature of investors. The market views firms headquartered in hard-currency countries as holding hard-currency assets, even if they allocated part of their assets in weak-currency countries. As a result, their earnings derived from weak-currency-denominated assets are capitalized at a higher rate. While this favors firms in hard-currency countries to acquire assets in weak-currency countries, it causes direct investment flows from the former to the latter. Aliber's approach provides a new perspective, and he also has a point in arguing that existing theories lack elements of "foreignness" (that is, they do not include the variables, such as different taxation, currency and customs zones, which differentiate national economies). However, in a strict sense an approach based on foreign-exchange and capital market imperfections is not a theory of foreign direct investment. Aliber does not show the necessity for direct investment, since the same benefits can be better obtained by a mutual fund invested in foreign capital markets. Why should there be foreign direct investment? Furthermore, Aliber's theory implies that direct investment is a country phenomenon because the arbitrage opportunity is available discriminatively and only available to all firms located in the hard-currency region. This is contradictory to the evidence that suggests that MNEs concentrate in industries with certain characteristics. Finally, the theory also cannot explain cross-country investment, which is reflected in the recent trend of international investment flows.

THE COMPARATIVE COST APPROACH

The orthodox approach to foreign direct investment inherits a framework from classical economics, with a critical basis on the assumptions of profit maximization and a perfectly competitive market. It renders an explanation of FDI flows when certain aspects of market imperfections are recognized. The explanations developed by Hirsch (1976) and Kojima (1978) exhibited a strong classical trace, with the analysis of the firm's choice of trade versus direct investment mainly based on the firm's comparative costs. These theories only provide a necessary but not sufficient condition for overseas investment undertaken by multinational enterprises. On the other hand, Horstmann and Markusen (1987) rationalized the issue by recognizing imperfect information for the buyer in the market.

Hirsch's Model Based on Comparative Costs

Hirsch (1976), while viewing exports, foreign production, and licensing as three alternative modes of foreign expansion, further considered the relative cost of these modes as a determinant of choice. First, the firm may produce in home country A and export to host country B, incurring home production cost P_A, domestic control cost C_D, and international marketing cost M_I. The firm could also choose to undertake production in host country B, incurring host production cost P_B, international control cost C_I, and domestic marketing cost M_D. Finally, the firm can transfer the know-how to a native firm in country B; then the native firm incurs production cost P_B, domestic control cost C_D, and fee to license know-how K. Assume that the international marketing cost is greater than the domestic marketing cost (the differential $\Delta M = M_I - M_D > 0$) and that the international control cost is greater than the domestic control cost (the differential $\Delta C = C_I - C_D > 0$). Consequently, export will take place if

$$P_A + \Delta M < P_B + K,$$

and

$$P_A + \Delta M < P_B + \Delta C.$$

That is, the sum of the home production cost and marketing cost differential is less than the sum of host production cost and licensing fee, and less than the sum of host production cost and control cost differential. Conversely, direct investment will take place if

$$P_B + \Delta C < P_B + K,$$

and

$$P_B + \Delta C < P_A + \Delta M.$$

That is, the sum of the host production cost and control cost differential is less than the sum of host production cost and licensing fee, and less than the sum of the home production cost and marketing cost differential.

Hirsch recognized the additional cost associated with foreign production. However, he developed a framework essentially on the premises of a perfectly competitive market but with a recognition of the costs of international activities. As a result, the theory does not provide a realistic explanation for the pattern of direct investment. For example, based on his model, licensing should always dominate foreign production and exports. That is because the control cost differential ΔC and the marketing cost differential ΔM are the expenditures resulting from the inefficiency of producing and selling in the foreign territory, which are the real, out-of-pocket costs. On the other hand, the licensing fee is the cost to the native firm but the revenue to the multinational firm. Based on his model, therefore, the multinational firm is always better off in licensing, and it will choose this strategy to transfer know-how to the native firm and receive the licensing fee in return. There should be no reason for the complication of foreign direct investment.

Kojima's Japanese-Type Foreign Direct Investment

The theory of foreign direct investment presented by Kojima (1978) is an extension of the classical economic paradigm of comparative costs. Kojima held that overseas investment may promote free trade and mutual prosperity only if it facilitates relocation of production corresponding to the international shift of comparative advantages. With that in mind, Kojima classified direct investment as the "American-type, anti-trade-oriented" and "Japanese-type, trade-oriented."

The argument is based on the observation that U.S. direct investment concentrates on the manufacturing industries generally associated with economies of scale, advanced technology, capital-intensive production, and marketing of differentiated products. According to Kojima, American corporations in these industries have comparative advantages and should serve foreign markets by exports. The aggressive investment expansion in these industries reflects the oligopolistic behavior of the firm and will only have a destructive effect on trade. On the other hand, the Japanese-type direct investment is undertaken mostly by small and medium-size firms, is targeted at developing countries, and occurs mostly in low-tech and labor-intensive industries. This type of direct investment leads to offshore production only in the sectors in which Japan no longer enjoys a comparative advantage but the developing countries may. This investment is complementary to Japan's comparative advantage and helps the adjustment of economic structure in Japan. Furthermore, it is also beneficial to the economy of host countries and helps them to achieve industrialization. In other words, Japanese-type investment promotes trade and the international division of labor.

Kojima's approach, based on a synthesis of the theories of trade and investment, explains primarily the earlier international expansion of Japanese firms and current foreign investment of firms based in newly developed countries such as Taiwan, Thailand and Hong Kong. However, with a framework built essentially on the classic economic paradigm, the explanation is limited. For example, Kojima advocates a shift of international production locations according to a shift of comparative advantage. However, the same shift of production location may well be accomplished by market exchange (in the absence of market imperfections). If a Japanese company loses a comparative advantage in certain production, why can't it simply license the technology or sell the production facilities to a native firm in the developing country? What do Japanese firms need to have direct control of foreign operations? In other words, Kojima does not show the necessity for foreign direct investment. Furthermore, today, Japanese companies' overseas investment presents a pattern similar to American-type foreign direct investment. For example, in a recent study based on a large sample of Japanese firms which have full or partially owned subsidiaries in the U.S., Hennart (1991) found that Japanese firms' decision on ownership form is determined by factors quite similar to those of U.S. firms. This confirms Mason's argument (1980) that the difference between American and Japanese overseas investment only reflects the different stages of the MNE institution's evolution.

The MNE's Reputation and Choice Between FDI and Licensing

Horstmann and Markusen (1987) developed a model to examine a firm's choice between FDI and licensing based on a recognition of the asymmetric structure of information in the market. When consumers cannot perfectly determine product quality prior to purchase, they judge quality based on previous purchase experiences. Here reputation plays a role. A multinational enterprise has a reputation for producing high-quality premium goods due to its possession of superior know-how. On the other hand, a native firm in a foreign country may only produce low quality goods. Faced with an opportunity to expand to a foreign market, the MNE can choose either direct investment or licensing. While the former earns the MNE operating profits, the latter lets the MNE receive royalties from a native firm that employs the MNE's know-how in local production. However, if the licensing strategy is chosen, since the production of high-quality goods is more costly and quality is unobservable, the moral hazards may occur—the native firm may sell the low-quality product under the guise of high quality and augment its short-term profit at the expense of the MNE's reputation. Therefore, the MNE must adopt a counter measure to discourage cheating, by offering the native firm a pecuniary incentive for maintaining quality. Furthermore, the value of this incentive should be greater than the gain from cheating. As such, it would be in the native firm's interest not to cheat. In this scenario, when the MNE has an overseas production cost identical to or less than that of the native firm, it will always prefer foreign production to licensing. When the MNE has a higher production cost, the choice is contingent upon the relative costs of foreign production and licensing—FDI will be chosen if the MNE's additional cost is less than the required pecuniary incentive, and licensing will be preferred if otherwise.

Horstmann and Markusen's study considers the choice between FDI and licensing as a dichotomy, which is determined by the relative costs of production under FDI and the moral hazards stemming from licensing. The choice arises because of the existence of market imperfections resulting from product differentiation and imperfect information. However, a theory based sheerly on a recognition of consumer market imperfection is inadequate to justify foreign direct investment. For instance, if a firm has a concern only on quality, it does not have to take foreign production. The firm can let the foreign native firm country undertake local production under licensing and exercise control over quality and market distribution. While this strategy can effectively restrain the moral hazards, it is pursued by major firms in the shoe and garment industries. In other words, Horstmann and Markusen still do not show the necessity of direct investment.

In summary, Hirsch, Kojima, Horstmann and Markusen and others limit their frameworks to consider only certain aspects of market impurities. This allows the complicated FDI phenomenon to become a manageable issue, and the elegance of the theory can be preserved. As such, however, the theories can only provide a limited explanation. A complete explanation of foreign direct investment and the multinational enterprise must belong to the market imperfection paradigm. Consequently, the industrial organization and internalization theories have to lead the way in explaining this international economic occurrence.

THE INDUSTRIAL ORGANIZATION APPROACH

The contemporary theory of foreign direct investment is based on the neoclassical approach, which holds the profit maximization assumption and explores the consequential behavior of the firm under imperfectly competitive market conditions. In this literature, foreign direct investment is considered as an instrument to overcome these market imperfections. More specifically, two aspects of market imperfections are emphasized. The structural imperfection approach considers FDI as the firm's strategic response to imperfect competition and relates it to firm-specific (monopolistic) advantages, market power, and the firm's anticompetitive behavior. On the other hand, the transactional imperfection approach focuses on the market hazards that prevent the market from being an efficient device to organize transactions. The first approach is established with a strong link to industrial organization economics and is the focus of discussion in this section. In the next chapter, we will turn to discuss transactional imperfection in the framework of the internalization theory.

The Industrial Organization Framework

Since industrial organization economics provides a conceptual basis for Hymer's and others' works, it is worthwhile to have a brief review of this literature. Industrial organization economics started to take shape between 1925 and 1950. In the early part of this century, U.S. industrialization led to rapid economic growth and creation of large industrial corporations, such as American Sugar Refining, General Electric, International Harvester, Standard Oil, and U.S. Steel. These companies commanded enormous wealth and were influential in U.S. society. General Motors, for example, was the world's largest company with sales equivalent to 3% of the U.S. gross national product (GNP) in 1955 and almost equal to the entire GNP of Italy for the same period. There was public concerned on such a concentration of economic power without public check and scrutiny. The issue, in particular, was how the "bigness" of business would affect production efficiency and economic welfare in terms of resources allocation and prices charged to consumers. As a response to this public concern, the industrial organization economics surged, providing a methodological approach to investigating the consequences of the firm's pursuit of its profitability objective.

The dominant approach of the industrial organization is the well-known structure-conduct-performance scheme summarized in Figure 2.3.[1] It suggests that basic supply and demand conditions, such as the way for raw materials to be sourced, the stage of technology, the price elasticity of demand, and the extent of substitute product availability, be conducive to the formation of a specific market structure. Market structure includes crucial elements such as seller and buyer concentration and entry barriers. The seller concentration is determined by the number and relative size of firms in the industry, and the barrier to entry—the advantageous position of established firms relative to new entrance—is substantial with the presence of product differentiation, economies of scale, the absolute cost advantage of the existing firms over new entrants, and the control of essential intermediate product supplies. Market structure has a strategic influence on the nature of competition and market consequence. As indicated in the scheme, market structure determines the firm's conduct—namely, the strategic behavior of the firm in pursuing its objectives. It influences the firms' pricing and product behavior, choice of R&D and advertising spending, and tactics to interact with competitors in the industry. Market structure directly and indirectly, through its effect on the firm's conduct, affects the industry performance, which is the outcome of business operations and is measured by the industrial profitability, efficiency of resource allocation, technological progress, employment, and so on. According to industrial organization economists, market structure determines and predicts the firm's conduct and industry performance. Furthermore, the outcomes may have feedback effects on the given determinants. As shown by the broken lines in Figure 2.3, the firm's conduct in turn may affect market structure and basic conditions. For example, the firms' intensive spending on R&D may lead to further product differentiation which results in enhancement of the entry barrier of the industry.

Figure 2.3
The Structure-Conduct-Performance Scheme

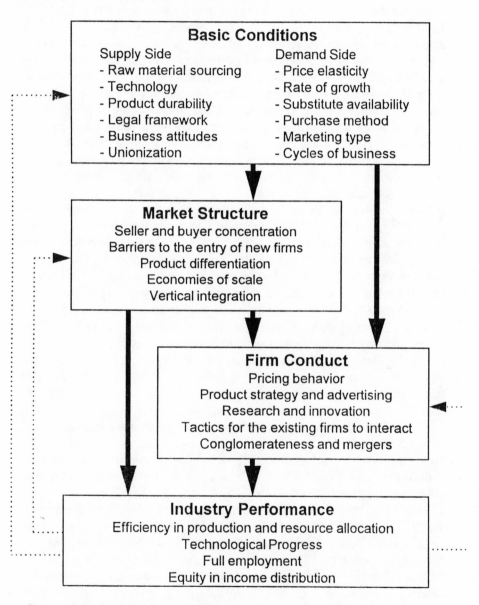

Source: Scherer, Frederic M. and David R. Ross, *Industrial Market Structure and Economic Performance* (1990), adapted.

The center of the analysis is how firms behave in the given market structure, with the basic premise that firms act to pursues their objectives of profit maximization. In the whole spectrum of economy, at one end there is the perfectly competitive industry, which consists of a large number of firms selling essentially undifferentiated products. Each individual firm essentially is a price taker, has no influence on the overall market performance, and earns zero economic profit. In this market situation, the analysis of the firm's conduct yields insignificant results. At the other end, there is monopoly, with one single firm dominating the whole industry. This is undesirable but is rarely seen in the private sector of the economy today. Between these two ends, there are industries that are formed by a varied number of firms. In an oligopolistic industry, a relevant market consists of a small number of large firms, with economies of scale, vertical integration, product differentiation and entry barriers all determining the outcome of industrial competition. In this market, market power is present—the leading firms have the ability to influence the market price perceptibly, and they will use the power to serve their profit objectives. With the oligopolistic market structure, there is mutual interdependence among existing firms. Consequently, an oligopolist will take into account not only the immediate market consequence of its actions but also the effects on other firms and their market reactions. For instance, each firm is fully aware that its initial price reduction will trigger similar reactions by other firms and, consequently, a price war, which eventually will hurt all firms in the industry. Therefore, their profit objectives can be better served through sellers' coordination, either by a formal agreement or tacit collusion. This strategy, however, often gives rise to the antitrust implication. One most recent case involves Archer Daniels Midland Co. (ADM), a major grain company, which pleaded guilty to the charge that it conspired to fix the global price for two agricultural commodities and agreed to pay a record fine of $100 million. Other companies involved in the case are all giants in the agricultural processing industry, including two Japanese companies, Kyowa Hakko Kogyo Company and Ajinomoto Company, and a Korean company, Sewon America.

Revealing results are further provided by Bain (1956, 1959) through the analysis of entry barriers to the industry. Bain considered entry barriers as a determinant factor of industrial performance, suggesting that only with the existence of substantial entry barriers can the firms raise their prices and profits without inviting new entrants to the industry, which otherwise would intensify competition and drive down industry profitability. His analysis was further given to the conscious attempt of existing firms to erect barriers to discourage the new entrance. One commonly used tactic is the merger or acquisition, which creates a new industry giant with a dominant market

Example 2.1 Kodak's Tactics: Mirror Image of Fuji's Conduct at Home?

Eastman Kodak Corporation, based in Rochester, New York, is a leading firm in the photography industry. In May 1995, it filed a petition with the U.S. Trade Representative Mickey Kantor, charging Fuji Photo Film Corporation with unfair dominance of Japan's market. The 300-page report claimed that Fuji blocked market access by controlling distribution through Japan's four biggest wholesalers (known as *tokuyakuten)* and retailers, offering them rebates and cash payments for selling only Fuji's products. As a result, concluded the petition, Fuji maintains a control of 70% of the Japanese market. Kodak, after investing $750 million, has only a slim 9% of the market there, with a loss of sales amounting to $5.6 billion over the past twenty years. The allegation activated an official investigation under Section 301 of the U.S. Trade Act, which gives the U.S. government the power to impose sanctions on foreign products and firms that are proven to damage American industry.

Minoru Ohnishi, president of Fuji Film, responded with fury, saying the accusations against his company were "complete fabrication" and "untrue, irresponsible and self-serving." Meanwhile, Bill Barringer, a Fuji lawyer, rebutted Kodak's market-share argument, pointing to Kodak's 70% of the U.S. wholesale photofinishing market—"using Kodak's logic one could make the case that the U.S. market is unfairly closed to Fuji Film thanks to Kodak's anti-competitive practices." Consequently, Fuji Film, with its investment of $2 billion, holds only 10% of the U.S. market. On July 31, 1995, Fuji filed with Kantor's office a 585-page report entitled "Rewrite the History," claiming that Kodak hogs its own domestic market. Specifically, Kodak gave U.S. retailers rebates and up-front payments to exclude competitors, and it secured exclusive accounts through ownership and by giving discounts, advertising, and promotion support. One such exclusive agreement Kodak has is with Eckerd Corporation, the country's fourth largest film outlet. Kodak also pays rebates in a significant amount to the Army and Air Force Exchange Service (AAFES) for exclusivity. An AAFES merchandise manager testified in court that the company would not have received the $2.7 million payment for the sales of 1991 if it had carried any brands other than Kodak. Because of Kodak's exclusionary practice, Fuji claimed to lose sales estimated to be over $4.5 billion in the last ten years.

"For Fuji to claim that what Kodak faces in Japan is the 'mirror image' of what Fuji faces in the United States is absurd," Kodak Chairman George Fisher declared. But the stories revealed by some U.S. photofinishers and retailers showed how forceful Kodak could be. To push them to drop other brands, it offered cash payments and expensive equipment and also threatened to delay services and remove the dealership. The battle between two giants is not over yet, and the case has been turned to the World Trade Organization. The accusations remain to be validated, but there is a resemblance in the alleged tactics—they are the firm's conscious efforts to block new entries and the firm conduct often observed in oligopolistic industries.

Sources: "Fuji, Accused by Kodak of Hogging Markets, Spits Back: 'You Too'," *The Wall Street Journal,* July 31, 1995, p. A1. "Fuji Denies Kodak Unfairness Accusation," *The New York Times,* August 1, 1995, p. D2. "Shattered," *The Economist,* August 5, 1995, p. 59.

share and enormous resources which deters other firms from entering competition. There are some other tactics used by established firms to discourage new entrance. Example 2.1 discusses the case of the photography industry, which has a high level of market concentration not often observed in some other industries. For example, Eastman Kodak controls 70% of the U.S. market and 40% of European markets, while its Japanese counterpart Fuji Photo Film holds a similar domestic market share. These oligopolists are formally accusing each other of anticompetitive behavior. The allegation includes tactics such as the demand for exclusive dealership to carry their products, up-front cash payments and cumulative rebates to retailers for the sales of products, and even coercive tactics. While these two oligopolists probably both are guilty of the charges, these practices resemble each other and are entry barriers in nature, which are often pursued by existing firms to enhance their positions and to discourage potential entrants to the industry (for a summary, see Sawyer 1981).

Traditionally, the industrial organization research develops its analysis with a major focus on the firms operating in a domestic setting. This field of study, "despite its tendency to ignore international influences on domestic product markets, offers a broad context in which to assess the significance of foreign investment" (Bergsten et al. 1978, p. 231). This theory is relevant to the occurrence of direct investment because the multinational enterprise prevails in the industries with a high market concentration ratio and with substantial entry barriers related to economies of scale, initial capital investment, and spending on research and development (R&D) and advertising.

The Hymer-Kindleberger Paradigm

Hymer (1976) started with an analysis of the distinguishing feature of the multinational enterprise—namely, its possession of firm-specific advantages. These advantages were further identified by Kindleberger (1969) as brand names and trademarks, management and marketing skills, patented and proprietary technology, access to low-cost capital, economies of scale, and so on. Johnson (1970) held that the primary basis of the firm-specific advantage is superior knowledge, which is firm specific and cannot be duplicated easily by others because of its proprietary nature or due to patent protection. Caves (1974, 1982) emphasized product differentiation, arguing that the multinational's possession of intangible assets allows it to differentiate products in the market and secure a time stream of cash flows. This knowledge-based advantage is often referred to as the firm's know-how intangible assets. The link between the firm's know-how superiority and the level of foreign involvement has been confirmed by prior studies.

Overwhelming evidence suggests that the firms aggressively seeking overseas investment generally are leading firms in their industries. They are large in size; spend more in research and development (R&D) and advertising; employ a higher proportion of scientists, engineers, and managerial and professional personnel; market some distinctive products; and have access to the market distribution network.[2]

The relationship between the firm's know-how intensity and foreign involvements is due to the "public good" characteristic of knowledge-based products; that is, the products can be used jointly. The creation of know-how is costly and requires intensive resource input. Once it has been developed, the marginal cost to apply it to additional production is very low, and this gives rise to multiplant economies of scale (Markusen 1984). Therefore, the firm with ownership of know-how actively seeks business expansion, replicating the existing production facilities and the use of know-how to maximize its profits. The Coca-Cola Company is an example—its most valuable asset is the possession of a secret formula to make a soft drink. With that proprietary information, it seeks to establish similar bottling plants in as many territories as possible, including those that happen to be overseas, to strive for higher profits. In other words, the multinational enterprise is only a special case of the multiplant firm, which seeks to extend the application of its know-how to operations in foreign countries.

The existence of firm-specific advantages by itself, however, is insufficient to explain foreign direct investment. This is because self-use is not the only way to exploit the benefits of firm-specific know-how overseas. Alternatives for international know-how transfer include various kinds of market arrangements. For example, a firm may license its know-how to a native firm in a foreign country and let it organize local production based on know-how. In return, the licensing firm will receive a part of profits in the form of royalty and licensing fees. Ideally, the market-based approach should be a more viable choice (because of the MNE's disadvantage operating in a foreign country and the additional cost resulting from this disadvantage). Therefore, the efficiency consideration would predict the predominance of the market mode in international know-how transfer. This, of course, contradicts the reality, which shows a strong tendency toward FDI and direct control. As such, one question can be raised: Given the apparent disadvantage of foreign production, why does FDI still dominate over licensing in a firm's choice? More specifically, why does the firm prefer self-use of know-how over selling it to a foreign firm? According to Hymer, the explanation is that the ideal situation for market exchange rarely exists and firms generally operate in a highly imperfect market.

Under the market conditions of imperfect competition, foreign direct investment becomes a more profitable means. The industrial organization theory, particularly Bain's work on entry barriers, provides great insights in this analysis. As indicated in the "structure-conduct-performance" scheme (Figure 2.3), the firm's conduct is a product of the market structure. Hymer, while noticing that FDI takes place mainly in highly concentrated industries, suggested that should be a strategy pursued by the oligopolistic firm to take advantage of structural market imperfections. The focus of analysis is the firm-specific advantage, which is a firm's certain ability not available to others and thus is monopolistic in nature. This advantage can be exploited overseas by licensing, but such a strategy is less desirable because it means relinquishing the firm's control of the advantage and the source of its market power. Only by direct investment, can the firm maintain its monopolistic advantages and ability to earn a return higher than that of its local competitor. Therefore, FDI is an oligopolist's action to take advantage of imperfections in the market structure.

The FDI strategy is further considered an instrument to enhance the firm's market power (e.g., an international merger can bring business firms of different nationalities and owners under common ownership and thus removes competition). Take Japan's giant Bridgestone Tire Company as an example. In 1982 it acquired the American company Firestone and created the third largest tire company in the world. This international acquisition not only improved the strategic position of the joint company but also resulted in higher market concentration and, structurally, a more imperfect market. In short, foreign direct investment is a strategic response of the firm to the structural market imperfections and the conduct of an international oligopoly to overcome competition and enhance its market power.

Alternatively, the MNE's foreign investment can be a pro-competitive force which promotes productive and allocative efficiency in the host country. As Caves (1971) suggested, the MNE's firm-specific advantage over the native firm endow it with better ability to overcome entry barriers in the host countries. This advantage may further enhance its ability to overcome barriers to exit the host market (Caves and Porter 1976).

Other Literature Based on Industrial Organization

The industrial organization framework provides guidance in examining a wide range of issues related to the multinational enterprise. Ray Vernon (1966) developed the product-cycle model to introduce trade and direct investment as different stages of a sequential development process. He suggests that products undergo predictable change in the location of production and direction of marketing. In the new product stage, an innovative product is likely to be introduced in the United States, where technology and economic development are more advanced. At this stage, production is unstandardized and cost is high, and the demand comes mainly from the U.S. domestic market, where consumers have higher income levels and their consumption needs are more sophisticated. When it comes to the maturing product stage, which is associated with production expansion, a certain level of standardization has been achieved. The United States will export certain products to other developed countries to meet the market needs there. Eventually, firms in these countries start to have local production, and U.S. firms will then move the production location there as a defensive strategy to secure the local market shares. When the standardized product stage is reached, production becomes highly standardized, and price is the major factor determining the competitive outcome. The firms from the United States and other developed countries will move labor-intensive production to developing countries where the labor cost is the lowest. At this stage, the consumption needs in the developed countries will mostly be satisfied by overseas imports. This theory can explain the international shifts of production location for products such as TV sets, calculators and other consumer electronics. The later work by Vernon (1974, 1979) further modified the product-cycle model with an emphasis on the oligopolistic structure of industries in which the multinational enterprise operates. Multinational enterprises are further classified as innovation-based oligopolies, mature oligopolies, and senescent oligopolies, with each firm consciously seeking to maintain its position in oligopolistic competition.

The oligopolistic nature of foreign direct investment is supported by a high association between market concentration and the multinationality of the firm. The early study by Dunning (1958) found that two-thirds of foreign subsidiaries in Britain operate in markets with a highly concentrated structure. A survey by Steuer et al. (1973) showed a significant correlation between seller concentration and share of foreign subsidiaries of UK industries. Similar findings were presented in studies based on the country data of France and West Germany (Fishwick 1981), Australia (Parry 1978), New Zealand (Deane 1970), Canada (Caves et al. 1980) and the United States (Pugel 1978). Lall (1979) investigated how the entry of foreign multinationals affects industrial concentration in host countries based on the data of Malaysian industries. Findings suggested that economies of scale, required capital investment, and product differentiation all represent entry barriers and promote market concentration. Furthermore, a cross-section analysis shows a positive association between the level of foreign presence and the degree of concentration. Foreign investment increases concentration partially because foreign entry introduces new processes and products, brings new technology, and raises the capital intensity of production.

Confirmation of an empirical link between oligopolistic structure and direct investment by no means has established a causal relation between these two variables. Strictly based on the methodology, we may not conclude that the industry structure is the cause or the consequence of the MNE's foreign investment. Thus, Knickerbocker's work (1973) provides a meaningful result. In a study of 187 major American corporations based on data from the Harvard Multinational Enterprise Study, Knickerbocker found that foreign expansions of major firms in oligopolistic industries present a certain pattern, with their times to enter each particular foreign country closely related. Moreover, the higher the degree of seller concentration, the more closely the leading firm's foreign entry is followed by other firms. The findings conclude that foreign direct investment exhibit the nature of oligopolistic response. This investment essentially is a defensive strategy—one firm's foreign entry is perceived as a disruption of the existing market balance and thus triggers similar actions by other firms, which are considered necessary to negate the first mover's gains from its foreign position. Flowers's study (1976) found that direct investment by firms in the highly concentrated European and Canadian industries has a tendency to come to the United States in clusters, apparently in response to a move of the leading firm. This result is consistent with Knickerbocker's study, suggesting that the investment of European and Canadian firms in the U.S. market follows a similar pattern of oligopolistic response.

Another important issue is how foreign direct investment affects the market structure of home and host countries. The study by Bergsten et al. (1978) focused on the consequences of foreign direct investment on the firm's market power in the context of home country. The findings concluded that the multinational's foreign investment reinforces its domestic market position through backward integration to cheap labor and raw materials, forward integration to new markets, spreading the fixed cost of R&D over a larger sales base, and risk reduction through international diversification. Their study also finds that firms with higher levels of direct investment tend to be more profitable in domestic operations, which supports the hypothesis that foreign direct investment has an impact on industry performance at home. Horst (1975) provided compatible evidence, showing that a firm's foreign investment leads to higher profitability in its domestic operations. In a study based on U.S. corporation data from 1965 to 1971, Gaspari (1983) found that the multinational's export activity has a consistently strong impact on domestic profitability while its foreign investment activity has an insignificant impact on performance at home. Other studies sought to examine the consequence of the MNE's expansion on the host market based on the data of Brazilian and Mexican industries (Connor 1977), and Canadian industries (Eastman and Stykolt 1967, Shapiro 1983). The results are not consistent. It appears that the nature of industries, the market structure before direct investment, and the host government policies all should be carefully assessed to determine the outcome of market performance.

In brief, a body of literature has been developed to examine the MNEs' foreign expansions. Overall, the industrial organization literature centers on the cause and consequence of foreign direct investment, and the results conclude with solid empirical evidence that a certain kind of market structure is conducive to the rise of multinational enterprises.

SUMMARY

Researchers develop theories of foreign direct investment to rationalize this international economic phenomenon. However, a theory can truly demonstrate the necessity of direct investment only if it explains (1) FDI as a mode of international production, (2) FDI as a substitute for trade, and (3) the economic rationale of FDI given the recognized inefficiency associated with this form of foreign involvement. Judged by these three criteria, some research cannot be considered an FDI theory. The industrial organization theory then is proposed as a major approach to explaining foreign direct investment.

The industrial organization research focuses on structural market imperfections as the major explanation for foreign direct investment. It suggests that the firm undertake direct investment to seek strategic gain in a market with imperfect competition. This investment allows the firm to have direct control over its firm-specific know-how employed abroad and secures it monopoly rent. It may further result in a market with more structural imperfections and enhance the firm's market power. A large body of empirical literature has been developed that generally provides supportive evidence. The findings suggest the existence of a statistical relationship between oligopolistic structure and direct investment, a consequential effect of the investment on the multinational enterprise's profitability, and oligopolistic interdependence exhibited in the FDI pattern. All these results are consistent with industrial organization and conclude the market power hypothesis. They render support to the notion that FDI is a strategic response of an oligopolistic firm and a vehicle employed by the firm to gain advantage from the structural market imperfections.

The industrial organization research has a strong empirical basis because of the high empirical content of the theory. This branch of economics was developed in the early part of the twentieth century in response to public concern about the social and economic consequences of industrial concentration, and it started with a strong empirical tradition. This merit has also extended to the research of the multinational enterprise, and thus it is relatively easier for the industrial organization approach to develop effective empirical models and designs to test the theoretical hypotheses. The empirical strength of this research is more evident when it is compared with the internalization literature, which is the focus of Chapter 3.

NOTES

1. The broad framework of these relationships is a product of research works of numerous scholars, including Edward S. Mason (1939), Richard B. Heflebower (1954), Joe S. Bain (1956, 1959), Steve H. Sosnick (1958), J. M. Clark (1961), Richard E. Caves (1964), and F.M. Scherer (1970).

2. There is ample empirical evidence of the relationship between a firm's multinationality and different measures of firm-specific advantages. See Vaupel (1971), Vernon (1971), Caves (1974), Buckley and Casson (1976), Denekamp (1995), Gruber et al. (1967), Wolf (1977), Bergsten et al. (1978), Dunning (1981), Hirschey (1981), Lee and Kwok (1988), and Morch and Yeung (1991).

3

Internalization Research
in Its Current State

In the search for a general framework, the internalization theory has emerged as a predominant approach to justifying multinational enterprises. This analysis, with its focus on transactional market imperfections, considers foreign direct investment as a substitute for market transactions and a device to overcome obstacles in international exchange. Buckley and Casson (1976) rendered a systematic analysis in the internalization framework with a basis on three key premises: (1) The firm operates in the market to maximize its profit; (2) the existence of market imperfections motivates the firm to bypass the market, replacing it by internalization and conducting transactions between parties under common ownership; and (3) the firm is multinationalized when internalization is extended across national boundaries. In this framework, the theory of internalization is viewed as an explanation for the existence of firms in general and a justification for multinational enterprises in particular.

A new generation of internalization emphasizes transaction cost economics. The original idea of transaction costs was found in Coase (1937) and was expanded by Arrow (1969), Williamson (1975), and others. An extension of the analysis to multinational enterprises was further presented by McManus (1972), Casson (1987), Hennart (1982), Rugman (1980, 1981), Teece (1981a, 1981b), and Dunning (1981). As a result, the internalization theory is restructured in the transaction cost framework, with the MNE being recognized as an economic institution that seeks transaction cost minimization through the choice of foreign entry modes. Specifically, it chooses between internalization and alternative market modes based on an assessment of costs and benefits related to each transaction mode. The significance of this modification is to provide a balanced approach to the

MNE's internal and external market operations. It thus rectifies early literature, which unduly emphasized the FDI part of the MNE's foreign expansion strategies. The power of the transaction cost approach lies in providing "a framework for discriminating between those transactions that need to be internalized and those that do not. Without such a framework, the internalization theory of the multinational enterprise must be considered incomplete, and perhaps even tautological" (Teece 1986, p. 25). With a foundation on transaction cost economics, the internalization theory truly establishes itself as a theory of multinational enterprise rather than a theory of foreign direct investment.

THE FRAMEWORK OF TRANSACTION COST ECONOMICS

The basic notion of transaction costs was first developed by Coase to address a fundamental issue: "why a firm emerges at all in a specialized exchange economy" (1937, p. 390). Notice that there are two alternative forms to coordinate production: One is the external market, which is decentralized and achieves resources allocation through the price mechanism; the other is the internal organization of the firm, which suppresses the price mechanism with central planning and direct control. Thus, the real question is: If the market can accomplish all the economic coordination, why is there a need for the firm? The explanation, according to Coase, is that "the operation of a market costs something and by forming an organization and allowing some authority (an 'entrepreneur') to direct the resources, certain market costs are saved" (1937, p. 392). The cost to use the market is further identified as the cost to discover the relevant price, cost of negotiating and concluding contracts, and uncertainty associated with contracts based on long-term commitment.

However, if the market has deficiencies and if some market costs can be saved through internalization, why should the market remain in existence? In other words, there could be a single large firm that directs all the activities of an economy. According to Coase (1937), it is because the internal organization of the firm also operates with costs, which are mainly associated with (1) the diminishing rate of return when a firm expands above a certain scale, and (2) inefficient allocation of resources resulting from the absence of a pricing mechanism to direct all economic activities. Similar ideas are further advanced by other authors. For example, Arrow (1969) considered the firm as a device developed to contain the cost to organize economic activity. Williamson (1975) examined thoroughly the deficiencies associated with the internal organization, with a particular consideration of the internal procurement bias, internal expansion bias, and program persistence bias.

Williamson (1975) developed the "Markets and Hierarchies" approach to examine the set of market modes and the hierarchial organization of firm as two alternative forms with which to organize transactions. In the ideal world without imperfections, there would be no cost to use either organizational form, and the choice would be a matter of individual preference (Hennart 1982). However, in reality both organizational modes are not perfect, and there are costs associated with the use of either mode to organize transactions. The cost to use the market stems from the interface between a set of environmental factors and a set of human factors. The environmental factors include uncertainty and a small number. While the former refers to the unpredictability of the world with the future outcome being affected by many unforeseen factors, the latter concerns the situation in which the market consists of only a limited number of participants. These factors, however, become a threat to the operation of the market only when human deficiencies, such as opportunism and bounded rationality, are present. Opportunism extends the basic economic assumption of self-interest pursuit by further suggesting that individuals pursue self-interest with guile. The concept of bounded rationality was first advanced by Simon, who suggested that "rationality is bounded when it falls short of omniscience. And the failures of omniscience are largely failures of knowing all the alternatives, uncertainty about relevant exogenous events, and inability to calculate consequences" (Simon 1979, p. 502). The interface of environmental and human factors poses serious market hazards, which can be examined in exploring the efficiency consequence of various transactions.

A case in point is asset specificity (Williamson 1985). An asset is specific when it, once being deployed, cannot be converted easily to some other uses or cannot be done without a substantial loss of value. This "lock-in" phenomenon, with the presence of opportunism, creates a deterrent for market transactions. One party may take advantage of the fact that it is costly for another party to withdraw from the relation. Thus, there is a need for certain safeguard measures. If all future incidents can be foreseen, the opportunistic behavior can be restrained by a well-written contract, which specifies a set of arrangements for all future circumstances. However, in a world with uncertainty, given the bounded rationality of human beings, it is difficult to write a contract comprehensive enough to encompass all future outcomes and provide protection to both transaction parties. Consequently, internal organization will emerge to deal with this type of transaction. When transaction parties are under common ownership, the incentive for one party to seek an unfair gain at another's cost will be significantly restricted.

The major conclusion of this analysis is that internal organization is relatively more efficient in arranging transactions that deal with complex and heterogeneous products, have a limited number of sellers and buyers, are subject to great uncertainty, and require long-term contracting. On the other hand, the market is more efficient for transactions of homogenous goods and involving a large number of sellers and buyers. In Williamson's organizational failure framework, when the internal organization is more efficient than the market, the failure of the market occurs. On the other hand, when the market is more efficient than the internal organization, the failure of internal organization occurs. This is because the relative efficiency of these transaction modes will determine which is to be used for each transaction. Therefore, the internal organization is expected to dominate the first type of transactions, and the market will prevail in the second type of transactions.

In current literature, the choice of organization mode is overwhelmingly examined in the transaction cost framework. The specific term "transaction cost" originally appeared in Arrow's writing (1969), and was defined as "the cost of running the economic system" (p. 48). Based on this framework, the choice of transaction mode for each specific transaction is to be made purely for "the purpose and the effect of economizing on transaction costs" (Williamson 1981, p. 1537). Thus, in an economy with competing modes of transactions, the least-transaction-cost mode will be chosen for each transaction. One important implication is that the firm will grow through internalization to an extent that the cost of internalization is equal to the cost of organizing the transaction through the market. Furthermore, when the relative costs to use various modes change, there should be a shift of emphasis.

In recent years, with expansion of the market, development of information technology and the trend of deregulation, the cost of using the external market for transactions should have been declining. Thus the theory predicts that certain transactions, which were formerly conducted through internalization, now should be externalized. This provides an explanation for the recent trend of corporate downsizing (e.g., companies terminate some full-time technical staff but hire them back as independent consultants to perform the same tasks, and big U.S. auto makers aggressively seek outsourcing of components and supplies). The efficiency implication of transaction mode choice is further exhibited by Taiwan's computer giant Acer Corporation. This firm has achieved phenomenal successes by aggressively externalizing much of its internal transactions, which is achieved by breaking up the company into separate business entities and allowing the lower-level managers to have substantial ownership participation. In short, the transaction cost economization is the driving force promoting current economic restructuring.

The application of transaction cost economics to multinational enterprises also generates revealing results and provides further understanding of the firm's foreign expansion. Teece (1981a, 1981b) first adopted the "Markets and Hierarchies" approach to explain the rise of the MNE and its choice between direct investment and market transaction modes for foreign entries. Subsequently, internalization has been presented in the transaction cost framework as the theory of multinational enterprise.

INTERNALIZATION APPROACH TO MULTINATIONAL ENTERPRISES

Buckley and Casson (1976) recognize modern production as a process that involves the participation or input of various units, with each specializing in a different aspect of economic activities, including manufacturing, marketing, research and development, human resources development, procurement, and management of financial assets. These units are interdependent and relate to each other by a flow of intermediate products. These intermediate products include materials, components and semi-finished goods, which are sometimes in tangible forms. More often they are in intangible forms and knowledge-based, encompassing elements such as patents, engineering expertise, management and marketing skills, and quality control. The efficiency consideration requires these economic flows to be organized as transactions. In many occasions, however, it is difficult to use the market to organize transactions of intermediate products. This creates an incentive for the firm to bypass the market. As such, the internal market is created by the formation of the firm, which unites different transaction parties under common ownership. When this internalization is extended across national boundaries by the means of foreign direct investment, another multinational enterprise is born.

The MNE institution can be classified as vertically integrated or horizontally integrated, and is defined mainly by the tangible nature of the major intermediate products to be internalized. The multinational enterprise is formed with a vertically integrated structure when it transfers through the internal market intermediate products mainly in the tangible form. This type of investment can be more often identified with the firms' foreign expansion in the early part of this century, which integrated backward to the countries that are sources of raw materials, such as oil, copper, and iron ore. On the other hand, the multinational enterprise is horizontally integrated when its creation of internal markets is mainly for the transfer of intangible intermediate products—namely, the know-how-based products. This type of firm invests abroad to duplicate production facilities in the home country and extend the use of know-how. An example is Citibank's decision to open a branch office in Shanghai, which resulted in an intrafirm transfer of personnel, financial know-how and resources there. Of course, both types of multinational enterprises have engaged in the intrafirm transfer of tangible and intangible products, but there are different levels of emphasis.

One major motivation for the firm to undertake vertical direct investment is to seek a stable supplier-user relationship across national boundaries. This investment allows the firm to extend ownership to the foreign base of resources and low-cost production and transfer through the internal market the intermediate products, such as raw materials, components, and semi-finished products. Backward-integration investment is popular in industries whose competitiveness critically depends on a cheap and reliable source of supplies. This investment is also sought when quality is a primary concern but is difficult for the buyer to determine before the purchase. Internalization enables the firm to establish quality assurance and brand names (Casson 1982). As Williamson (1985) emphasized, without transactional market imperfections, the firm may simply use long-term contracts to establish supply sources and avoid the burden of direct investment.

Horizontal foreign direct investment is undertaken by the firm to seek multiplant expansion and is mainly involved with an intrafirm transfer of technical know-how, such as engineering skills and administrative and marketing expertise. Its relevance to know-how transfer is further evidenced by a strong empirical link between the firm's multinationality and its ownership of, and capability to produce, superior knowledge. To justify the firm's preference of internalization to the market for international know-how transfer, Hymer provided two reasons: (1) the firm's direct control and use of know-how can bring in more profits when the market presents imperfect competition, and (2) the existence of market impurities makes the market inefficient to organize market transactions of know-how. The first explanation recognizes the monopolistic nature of firm-specific know-how and considers FDI as a firm's strategic action to maintain and enhance its market power (which is discussed in the industrial organization framework of Chapter 2). The second explanation concerns the transactional market imperfections—namely, various obstacles to market transactions. Hymer then elaborated on the second point:

The owner of advantage may use it himself because his evaluation of it is different from the evaluation of other people because he has more information about his advantage and a greater incentive to use it. Aside from causing a conflict of evaluation, uncertainty makes it difficult for buyers and sellers to achieve a satisfactory licensing contract. . . . A reluctance to license may also arise from inherent danger of losing the advantage. (Hymer 1976, p. 50)

This discussion has identified the underlying causes for market failure, suggesting that it is difficult to organize know-how transfer in the market because of (1) asymmetric information between the buyer and seller, (2) the uncertainty associated with know-how application, and (3) the incentive to preserve the proprietary nature and thus the pecuniary value of know-how. While these basic ideas appear in the subsequent literature, they are elaborated in a refined and more rigorous fashion and presented as new theories of the multinational enterprise.

Prior literature (e.g., Arrow 1962, Johnson 1970, Magee 1977) extensively discusses market failure associated with know-how transactions based on recognition of the "public-good" nature of knowledge-based products. Hennart (1985) provided a thorough analysis of market transactions of know-how and identified the obstacles in the forms of information, enforcement and bargaining costs. The know-how product has the characteristic of public good in the sense that it is indivisible and can be used by others without excluding its availability to the original owner. However, when it is available to all others, the private return to the owner will be zero. To illustrate these points, we suppose that there is an auto manufacturer, whose major competitiveness lies in the possession of know-how to produce a high-quality engine. The know-how advantage is considered the firm's intangible asset which allows the firm to sell its products at a premium price. This property has features different from the firm's other tangible assets such as land, plants and equipment. While exclusivity is the nature of tangible assets—its use is limited to one party—know-how and its benefits can be shared with others. The problem with that approach is that, if all other manufacturers have learned how to produce quality products, the owner of know-how can no longer charge a premium on its products. In other word, know-how would not bring any value to the firm. Therefore, the firm has a strong incentive to protect the proprietary nature of know-how. While this approach is in the best interest of the firm, it is undesirable from the societal perspective. For the society, the most economical approach is to make know-how available to all (since know-how, given its public-good nature, can be applied to additional production at a low marginal cost). However, that would deprive the incentive for the private sector to create new know-how. To encourage knowledge development, therefore, the government allows the know-how creator to have a temporary monopoly and also provides legal protection to the intellectual property right.

This legal protection, however, is difficult to enforce sometimes. As Arrow (1962) suggested, the property right for know-how should not always be easy to define (that is why there are so many legal disputes over intellectual property rights, and Example 3.1 presents one such case in the semiconductor industry). Thus it is difficult for the owner of know-how to maintain its monopolistic advantage for a long period. This is the appropriability problem associated with know-how; that is, it is difficult for the owner of know-how to retain all the pecuniary value of know-how, given

Example 3.1 Legal Battles on the Ambiguity of Intellectual Property Rights

On May 12, 1997, Massachusetts-based Digital Equipment Corporation abruptly filed a lawsuit against Intel Corporation, the semiconductor industry leader, accusing it of deliberately infringing on Digital's patented technologies. Specifically, Digital alleged that Intel unlawfully incorporated into its Pentium microprocessors three key technological elements, branch prediction, cache management, and high-speed instruction processing, developed by Digital engineers. Digital sought to stop the Pentium line and asked for unspecified damages.

Robert B. Palmer, Digital's Chairman revealed that Digital approached Intel in 1990 and offered to license the Alpha chip to Intel as its next-generation architecture. As a common practice, Digital also presented Alpha's blueprints. Then in late 1991, Intel formally rejected the offer. Two years later, Intel introduced its best-selling Pentium chips. Palmer said that he became suspicious when Intel's chief executive, Andrew S. Grovey, was quoted to say, "Now we're at the head of the class, and there is nothing left to copy." The subsequent investigation confirmed his original suspicion. Because the evidence is convincing enough, Digital decided to resort to this legal action. Intel was caught by surprise because it had never been approached for the dispute prior to the suit. Digital said that it did not want to alert its opponent, which might engage in legal maneuvers to delay the court actions. On May 14, Digital ran a full-page advertisement in *The Wall Street Journal* and *The New York Times* under the title "A Message to Digital Customers," justifying its lawsuit against Intel.

Some industry analysts viewed Digital's lawsuit as a move of desperation after years of disappointing results in seeking a comeback in the industry. However, Richard Belgard, a semiconductor consultant, after examining Digital's patents, believed that Digital had some grounds. He said that Intel's approach in dealing with the bottleneck of microprocessor design greatly resembles Digital's. Intel, while denying any wrong doing, vowed to vigorously defend itself. Experts suggested that a host of legal options were available to Intel. Intel made a plain remark on its portfolio of over 3,000 approved patent rights and hinted a countercharge on Digital's patent infringement. It could also argue that Digital improperly received overly broad patents for its design.

Litigation is recurrent in the industry. Intel just finished its own seven-year legal battle against Advanced Micro Devices, which ended with the permission for AMD to clone Intel's chip and AMD's agreement to pay Intel $58 million. When Microsoft launched its Windows NT operating system, Digital threatened to sue Microsoft for patent infringement, but this dispute resulted in a partnership between the two firms. Coincidentally, two days after Digital sued Intel, Cyrix Corporation also announced its lawsuit against Intel on patent infringement. Underlying all these nasty legal battles is the ambiguity of intellectual property rights. If the domain of knowledge goods could be clearly defined, much of these costly troubles could be saved.

Sources: "Suit by Digital Says Intel Stole Pentium Design," *The New York Times*, May 14, 1997, p. D1. "Digital Files Big Patent Suit Against Intel," *The Wall Street Journal*, May 14, 1997, p. A3. "Intel Expected to Face Little Damage From Suits," *The Wall Street Journal*, May 15, 1997, A3. News releases in Digital Equipment Corp.'s World Wide Web site.

the public-good nature of know-how. For example, the idea of the spreadsheet program originated with Dan Bricklin, a Harvard business student, who, with his friend Bob Frankston, developed a program called VisiCalc for Apple II computers in 1978. It was an instant success. Since then, however, there has been a proliferation of spreadsheet products: Lotus-123, Excel, Quattra, etc. Their producers borrowed the original idea but extended, modified, and refined the products, and competed directly with VisiCalc, which eventually disappeared from the market. The appropriability problem has been well recognized by the know-how creator, who, to maintain its advantageous position, must differentiate his/her products continuously by improving the product features (even if sometimes it means superficial modification). Another important implication of the analysis is that the firm may underinvest in less complicated know-how since the appropriability problem is more serious for this type of know-how.

Magee (1977) further extended the analysis to the multinational enterprise. The prominent feature of this economic institution is its possession of, and its ability to develop, knowledge-based products. Given the public-good nature of know-how, the firm is motivated to extend its production facilities and replicate the use of know-how to maximize its returns from the creation of know-how. In the international setting, the firm further has a strong tendency for self-use of know-how to preserve its proprietary nature and attenuate the appropriability problem. Foreign direct investment allows the firm to appropriate the know-how through internalization and reap higher value from its possession.

Market failure occurs as a result of bounded rationality, opportunism, and information asymmetries associated with transactions of know-how products (Arrow 1962, Williamson 1975, 1985), and its implications also shed light on the multinational enterprise (Teece 1977, 1981). If the know-how products were traded under perfect market conditions, with numerous buyers and sellers, divisibility of goods, and both buyers and sellers having equal access of information, the price would be established through competitive bidding, at a level where the marginal benefit equals the marginal cost. At that price, the firm will be indifferent to the choice between the market transfer and internalization. However, in reality the market is far from perfect, and there are formidable obstacles to market transactions, which are present in three aspects of transaction organization: recognition, disclosure and team organization.

First, there are obstacles associated with recognition, which refers to the process to identify and connect all buyers and sellers in the market. It is a costly and time-consuming process particularly when transactions involve sophisticated know-how products. From the buyer's perspective, there is a need to find all available alternatives with their technical specifications.

Afterward, it is the task to decipher and absorb all the information, which then provides critical input for rational decisions. However, given the human deficiency of bounded rationality, it is impossible to identify all the choices and process all the information. Furthermore, there is uncertainty associated with people's inability to foresee all future market outcomes, and the buyers' limited ability to digest the knowledge transferred. As such, it is difficult for the buyer to establish a fair view of the know-how supplies. In such a setting, the buyer engages with the seller in the negotiation process to drive for a bargain and develops a contract to protect his or her interest and ensure compliance with the terms of the contract. From the seller's perspective, there is an urgent need not only to identify all prospective buyers, but also inform them about his or her products, and conclude transactions with fair return from sales. If the seller could find a way to attenuate information asymmetry between the buyer and seller, the buyer uncertainty, and thus the transaction cost, would be substantially reduced. Information disclosure, however, often fails to correct the information problem in the transactions involving know-how products.

In our analysis of the cost to acquire and process information, we have presumed that all information is available in the market. The fact, however, is that information is not always available to all parties, and the asymmetric structure of information sustains in the know-how market while the seller is incapable of conveying all information to the buyer. This information imperfection exists mainly due to the opportunistic nature of human behavior. The situation can be illustrated by a comparison of market transactions of different products. Suppose that an individual owns a piece of property and has the intention to sell it. The owner, while knowing the value of this property, seeks to sell it at a full price. This will be possible only if the buyer is aware of all benefits of the asset. When it is a transaction of some tangible property, the seller should be willing to reveal all information, educating the seller through verbal communication and physical demonstration. This is a case in which information disclosure meets both parties' interests and promotes the transaction. On the other hand, if a transaction involves know-how products, information disclosure may cause a serious problem, as a result of the special nature of knowledge goods—"its value for the purchaser is not known until he has the information, but then he has in effect acquired it without cost" (Arrow 1971, p. 152). With the presence of opportunism, there is an unsurmountable obstacle known as the "fundamental paradox" of information. To facilitate transactions, the seller needs to provide information to the potential buyer, but the seller's disclosure may destroy the basis for exchange as it also provides an opportunity for a free ride. The buyer may take advantage of disclosure to obtain information rather than for making purchase decisions. However, if the seller, with the concern on know-how ownership, does not provide disclosure prior to purchase, the buyer is not informed enough to effectively evaluate the product. Then he or she may not be willing to pay the asked price, suspecting the seller of overstating the claim. In conclusion, the special nature of information goods, coupled with opportunism, presents a serious obstacle for market transactions of know-how.

The disclosure problem can be corrected if know-how is ex post observable—that is, benefits from the use of know-how are verifiable by a third party. Then a contingent contract can be established between the buyer and seller (Arrow 1971, Meade 1971). In a guarantee-type agreement, the seller will explicitly state the benefits from the application of know-how, and the market price is established based on the claim. Should the outcome deviate from the claim, the seller will be penalized. Contingent contracting will induce truth telling on the seller's part, and the market transactions can proceed efficiently. This approach is efficient because it creates no social cost and results in an equilibrium indistinguishable from that under perfect information (Spence 1976). This approach, however, may not be applicable to transactions associated with uncertainty, as in know-how transfer. The outcome of know-how application is determined by many circumstantial conditions, including environmental and human factors. Given the uncertainty involved, with the assumed risk-averse nature, the seller may not want to be bound by contingent contracting (Caves 1982).

Finally, there is difficulty in team organization for know-how transfer. The know-how products are developed with extensive input of human capital. The transfer of the hardware part of know-how should be easier to accomplish, but the transfer of the human aspect of know-how is always more difficult. Therefore, it may be a relatively simple task when the transfer involves know-how products such as a chemical formula and computer software. On the other hand, it would be more complicated to transfer know-how products that have high tacit contents and are not easily codified (Kogut and Zander 1993). This transfer process requires intimate personal contact, demonstration, and team development and depends more on the qualifications of the transferee staff. There are know-how transfer projects, particularly to developing countries, which fail to reach the designed standards and objectives, mainly because of a lack of qualified technical personnel. With the difficulty of transferring the human kind of know-how, some oil-producing countries in the Middle East, after nationalization of Western oil companies' assets in the 1950s, still retained the expatriates of these companies to run the operations.

With all the obstacles to using the market for know-how transactions, there is an economic incentive for substituting the market by internalization and transferring know-how within the organization. This approach then saves the firm the market transaction cost, but it will also incur the cost of internal organization. While the relative costs of different organizational modes vary for transactions of different know-how products, cost minimization is an overriding consideration in determining the firm's choice of mode for each know-how transfer. When the know-how product has less complexity and the property right is easier to define, the market will be relatively more efficient. A firm is likely to transfer its know-how through the market, for example, by licensing a specific engineering design to another unrelated firm. On the other hand, if the know-how is more complex and the knowledge is more proprietary in nature, internalization will be preferred. The firm will then extend ownership to different production locations and have direct control over know-how application.

The economic incentive for internalization also provides an explanation for multinationalization of the firm. Internalization is a preferred approach to exploiting foreign opportunities because the international market is likely to be more imperfect than the domestic market (Rugman 1980). By undertaking foreign direct investment, the firm extends its internal organization to foreign locations and organizes international know-how transfer between business entities under common ownership. In the transaction cost framework, the multinationalization of the firm's operation is a process in which "(1) firms choose the least cost location for each activity they perform, and (2) firms grow by internalizing markets up to the point where the benefits of further internalization are outweighed by the costs" (Buckley 1988, p.2).

ECLECTIC THEORY AND FIRM-SPECIFIC ADVANTAGES

An alterative to the internalization theory is Dunning's eclectic theory (1979, 1988), which suggests that the firm-specific advantage, internalization advantage and location advantage are three necessary and sufficient conditions for foreign direct investment. This theory seeks a reconciliation of different schools by presenting a synthesis based on major literature in industrial organization, market failure and location economics. This approach provides justification for direct investment by addressing three critical issues. The first issue was originated by Hymer (1976)—given the additional cost associated with foreign production, how can multinational enterprises compete with native firms in a foreign country? Ownership of firm-specific advantage is the explanation, which enables the MNE to offset the disadvantages of operating abroad. The second question then follows: Why doesn't the MNE, for the sake of saving additional costs, pursue a licensing strategy to exploit opportunities in the foreign market? Dunning refers to the internalization theory for an answer, suggesting that FDI is a solution to market failure, and internalization of international economic activities result in efficiency gains. Finally, where would the MNE go for foreign production? The location theory suggests that the MNE would choose the foreign markets where it can obtain economic gains by integrating its firm-specific advantage with local endowments. By asserting issues of "how," "why," and "where" in explaining the firm's foreign expansion, the eclectic theory explains and predicts the pattern of foreign direct investment.

The eclectic theory and internalization theory are essentially based on the same framework, and their analyses of the MNE generate similar points. The resemblance of these two is further shown by the similar empirical designs used by them to test their theories. However, Dunning's theory elegantly repackages the framework and decomposes a complicated issue into manageable questions. The elaboration based on the interface of firm attributes, nature of transactions and attractiveness of locations provides the economic rationale for foreign direct investment. Consequently, this school of thought is well received.

The theory of foreign direct investment based on the firm-specific advantage, however, has been opposed by some scholars. Casson and Buckley in different writings both argue that the internalization advantage itself can justify the investment. Consequently, the firm-specific advantage is sufficient but not necessary to explain the MNE's operations and thus should not be included as an element of the FDI theory. This view is further supported by other authors. Some arguments, however, merely reflect the variation in the meanings of the terms used in debate. This reminds us of Coase's warning:

Economic theory has suffered in the past from a failure to state clearly its assumption. Economists in building up a theory have often omitted to examine the foundation on which it was erected. This examination is, however, essential not only to prevent the misunderstanding and needless controversy which arise from a lack of knowledge of the assumption, but also because of the extreme importance for economics of good judgement in choosing between rival sets of assumptions. (1937, p. 386)

Clearly, a productive discussion must be based on the clearly defined and generally agreed connotation of terms. In the internalization framework, the term *firm-specific advantage* refers to the advantage such as proprietary know-how, which is available only to specific firms and thus monopolistic in nature, and the term *internalization advantage* refers to the advantage enjoyed by all firms with direct investment over those without (Casson 1987). If these terms are *not* used in the same context, disagreement is likely to occur. One such example can be found in Itaki's paper

(1991) which rejects the firm-specific advantage as an element of the MNE theory. He argued that since the internalization advantage is the source of firm-specific advantage, there should be "no place left to be filled by the 'ownership advantage' [firm-specific advantage]" (Itaki 1991, p. 450). This argument is logical on the surface. If a firm's ability to create advanced technology is derived from its "organizational power of internalization and integration," then the organizational power should be the underlying competitive advantage of the firm. Notice, however, a different meaning is given to the term used in the discussion. Itaki considers the internalization advantage to be a firm's superior ability to operate internal organization. He may be right that this internalization power is the determinant of firm-specific advantages. He is also arguably right that such internalization ability varies across firms (otherwise all firms would have the same technology). However, since this ability is different among firms, it is not an internalization advantage but a firm-specific advantage (i.e., the administrative skill). Therefore, based on Itaki's argument, the validity of the firm-specific advantage concept still cannot be rejected.

On the other hand, there are some compelling arguments used by some authors to refute the necessity of firm-specific advantage. Casson (1987) suggested that a firm will undertake FDI as long as the total benefit from it is greater than the total cost. Since this benefit can be from sources other than the firm-specific advantage, it is not crucial to include this advantage in the theory. To prove the point, Casson presented one example. Suppose there are two firms located in two countries, with one in the mining industry and the other in the mineral processing industry. If the corporate income taxes are not harmonized between these two countries, a merger between these two firms will generate profit gains, by manipulating transfer pricing to minimize joint tax liabilities. As the argument goes, the benefit from internalization, or the advantage enjoyed by the MNE over the native firm, plus the location factor, is adequate to motivate foreign direct investment. Consequently, the existence of firm-specific advantage is not necessary.

Neither Casson's argument nor his example is convincing. Conceptually, all firms are internalizers, formed to exploit the internalization gain at least in the domestic context. With the existence of an opportunity to internalize transactions across national borders, some choose to pursue it and others do not. Why is there such a difference? If the internalization advantage is the full explanation of FDI—that is, FDI occurs as long as the internalization gains are greater than the costs—then all firms should have an equal opportunity and ability to become multinational. As indicated in Casson's example, the opportunity for international tax arbitrage, if it exists, should be accessible to all firms. The next question is, Why don't all firms go for this opportunity? The answer may be that some firms choose not to because they are not competitive enough to face rivalry in the foreign market (if all firms have the opportunity and exercise the option, then all firms become multinationals and compete head on in global scope). This, of course, does not happen. This may be because individual firms have different abilities to tap the benefits of internalization and they subsequently choose different levels of multinationality. Either way, an ultimate question can be raised: Why is there a cross-firm difference in the ability to compete or tape the internalization opportunity? This brings the analysis back to the original point—firms vary in strength or capability to exploit the internalization advantage, and this cross-firm variation, by definition, is the firm-specific advantage.

A rejection of the firm-specific advantage contradicts the evidence that suggests a link between various measures of firm-specific advantage and the multinationality of the firm. It is also difficult to explain the pattern of vertical direct investment. If internalization advantage is the only required condition, then the direction of vertical integration is a discretionary choice. Since all firms have an equal ability to explore the internalization gains, it would be equally beneficial whether a mining firm integrates forward to processing or the metal firm integrates backward to extraction. Furthermore, forward integration by a banana plantation in South America to the U.S. consumer market should have the same effect as backward integration by an American market distributor to the source of supplies. Of course this is not a general case in reality. The evidence suggests that vertical investment normally is originated by the firm with a specialty in the stage based on more sophisticated know-how and leads to backward or forward integration to the stages requiring less sophisticated know-how.

Originally, the firm-specific advantage was identified by Hymer (1976) to explain the occurrence of foreign direct investment despite the additional cost associated with this investment. Therefore, a rejection of the firm-specific advantage must be preceded by a rejection of the additional cost postulation. This logic was clearly established by Casson:

Dunning implicitly retains the assumption that the MNE incurs additional costs of doing business abroad. But this assumption is no longer crucial because these costs are simply one component of the total cost of integrating activities in different countries, and it is only the overall cost that is crucial to the theory. Likewise it is unnecessary to retain the postulate that an MNE possesses an ownership advantage such as a superior technology because the benefits of internalization are themselves sufficient, in principle, to outweigh the cost of internalization and so make integrated operation profitable. (Casson 1987, p. 35)

A categorical denial of the additional cost concept is not desirable. This cost should exist logically and can be observed in practice. Logically, when we distinguish between the MNE and national firm, we mean that they are different. The differences should include both advantages and disadvantages. If there are only advantages associated with multinational operations, there would be no national firm left. On the other hand, if this operation has only disadvantages, this institutional form would never arrive in the first place. In practice, the additional cost is also a matter that cannot be simply ignored. To reject the relevance of the additional cost concept, Buckley (1985) further argued that it may exist but declines when a firm becomes more experienced in foreign operations. The argument is correct if he refers to the cost of control, communication, and operations in an unfamiliar environment. However, there are also costs in other forms which are not functions of the learning curve. For example, if investors perceive more risk (e.g., political risk) associated with foreign involvement, they will demand a corresponding risk premium in the required rate of returns. This

Table 3.1
Labor Cost and Labor Productivity of Foreign-Owned and American Domestic Manufacturing Firms Operating in the United States

	1988	1989	1990	1991
Labor Cost				
Production wage rates per hour (dollars)				
Foreign	11.84	12.08	12.57	12.88
U.S.	11.57	11.81	11.04	11.33
Foreign/U.S. (%)	112	112	114	114
Labor Productivity				
(1) Value added per production-worker hour (dollars)				
Foreign	70	73	74	77
U.S.	49	51	52	54
Foreign/U.S. (%)	142	144	140	141
(2) Output per production hour (dollars)				
Foreign	161	169	173	177
U.S.	104	108	112	116
Foreign/U.S. (%)	155	157	154	153

Source: U.S. Department of Commerce, Bureau of Economic Analysis, *Survey of Current Business* (1996).

represents an additional cost because a higher discount rate is used in the valuation of foreign cash flows. This additional cost will further be recognized in the social context, with acknowledgement of public rejection of foreign ownership and the subsequent policies developed by host governments which are unfavorable to the operations of foreign MNEs. This phenomenon has even been observed in the United States.[1]

There are many social spectrums which all can be transformed into the additional cost consequence. One example is the higher labor cost incurred by the MNE operating in the host country. The statistics have shown that the foreign multinational consistently pays a higher wage and salary than the local firm, which is the case even for an industrialized country such as the United States.[2] The higher pay should not be viewed as a foreign firm's generosity to citizens of the host country but as a compensation for all the negative connotations of working for a foreign firm; thus it represents the additional cost of foreign production. Alternatively, it may also be argued that workers in the foreign firm receive higher pay because they can perform more efficiently. However, this exactly is the point: The MNE's additional cost is offset by its firm-specific advantages. As revealed in Table 3.1, The productivity gain of Americans working for foreign firms in the United States are more than offset by the additional pay they receive from the firms.

One reason for the controversy over the additional cost concept is that it cannot be tested empirically. An alterative approach would be to direct an indirect test of the concept. Suppose that such a cost does not exist, then international and domestic acquisitions should present similar patterns, as Dewenter (1995) argues. Her recent study on the U.S. chemical industry suggests that foreign firms are more likely than the U. S. firms to make acquisitions in related industries, indicating that foreign investors may face a cost disadvantage which is severe enough to affect the international investment pattern. In conclusion, the additional cost exists in reality and should not be assumed away for simplification or elegance of the model. The significance of this cost may be different for different firms, as Buckley suggested (1985). However, this should not be an annoying factor but a determinant which systematically differentiates MNEs from national firms. With this cost varying across countries, firms with different levels of firm-specific advantages may choose different levels of multinationality (while the domestic firm can be considered a special case with the level of multination-ality equal to one). Consequently, there are separate equilibriums of foreign direct investment among firms.

A CRITICAL ASSESSMENT OF INTERNALIZATION

The internalization paradigm has gained great popularity in the last two decades, and notable supporters include Casson, Buckley, Dunning, Hennart, Magee, Rugman, and Teece and others. Today, it has become a mainstream research paradigm dominating major publications. If the rule of the majority were the basis for theory choice, then internalization would undoubtedly be the general theory of the multinational enterprise. However, such a selection criterion would contradict the believed objectivity of scientific knowledge. It is based on such a belief that researchers advance the research process—first a theoretical framework is presented, which is followed by sort of empirical evidence, which then is elaborated to make interpretations and conclusions. According to a positivist view, any theory, no matter how appealing or rigorous, must have an empirical basis. This view directs researchers to pay more attention to test results and the derived conclusions than to the assumptions. Therefore, it is also appropriate for us to judge the research accomplishments in the positivist framework.

The positivist approach is attractive further because it provides general rules for an objective appraisal of FDI theories. According to the methodology of scientific research programs (MSRPs) presented by Lakatos (1970), a research program should be assessed on whether the research series leads to progressive problemshifts or degenerating problemshifts. The program is progressive theoretically if it leads to discovery and explains novel facts, and it is also progressive empirically if it generates new postulation that can be confronted by evidence and results in consistent enhancement of empirical content. Lakatos's emphasis is on the empirical basis of programs because "the only relevant evidence is the evidence anticipated by a theory, and empiricalness (or scientific character) and theoretical progress are inseparably connected" (1970, p. 123). On the other hand, a research program is degenerating when "theories are fabricated only in order to accommodate *known* facts" (Lakatos 1974, p. 8). Lakatos further maintained that "if the reduction of the theory to the 'metaphysical' framework does not produce new empirical content, let alone novel facts, then the reduction represents a degenerating problemshift, it is a mere linguistic exercise" (1970, p. 126). Therefore, the performance of a particular research program can be judged by determining whether it leads the way to progressive or degenerating problemshifts.

In the Lakatosian scenario, the literature on the multinational enterprise can also be assessed. In the last two decades the internalization literature has presented a clear tendency of degenerating progress. This does not mean that this research has not produced worthwhile works. Although Hymer's original contribution is undisputable, other scholars, such as

Buckley and Casson, Dunning, Hennart, Magee, Rugman, and Teece, all significantly advanced the research in this area. In their initial writing, these authors presented fresh views and insights on the multinational enterprise, promoting the rigor of the theoretical structure, stimulating interest, and furthering our understanding of the issue. The problem is the direction of that research. The subsequent works of some authors, probably motivated by the aspiration to build a general theory, become less meaningful and significant overall. Much of their later publication presents not only a form of rhetoric but also consistently diminishing empirical content. The self-perpetuation of this research can be called the "immiserized growth of internalization." Casson's criticism of this literature is as follows:

Some of the authors direct too much effort into artificially differentiating their theories from others, and spend too little time on original analytical development. The same concept appears in different guises in different theories, so that the essential simplicity and parsimony of the conceptual framework is lost in the proliferation of rival jargon. (1987, p. 32)

A similar pattern, however, is also exhibited in Casson's own writing. For example, much of his criticism of others' works lacks empirical implications and in a sense is a matter of "linguistic exercises." His rejection of the firm-specific advantage concept is another form of "artificially differentiating" his theory. Despite his strong position, it is evident from his original work (e.g., Buckley and Casson, 1976) that this concept is also a key element in the internalization framework. The resemblance between internalization and eclectic theory is further evidenced by the similarity of empirical designs employed in their studies. The only difference is in interpretation—authors of different schools all seek to explain the results in the context of their own theories.

The development of eclectic theory can be cited as another example of immiserized growth. When the theory was first proposed, it was appealing for its simplicity and empirical promise. However, Dunning's later modifications (e.g., 1988), as a response to the criticism and an endeavor to construct a general theory, evolve to a framework that provides more flexibility but is infinitely irrefutable. Kogut and Zander's work (1993) is one more example. Their major argument is that market failure is not necessarily a cause for internalization. Apparently, there is a difference in understanding the concept of market failure—while Williamson considers that organizational failure exists when "the frictions associated with one mode of organization are prospectively attenuated by shifting the transactions, or a related set of transactions to an alternative mode" (1975, p. 20), Kogut and Zander *appear* (since they did not clearly define the term in the text) to consider market failure as a complete breakdown of the market.

Confusion over the meaning of some key economic terms should not deserve another academic debate.

An overview of internalization literature shows the trend of diminishing empirical content in the research. The so-called new theories do not generate predictions that are unknown and empirically progressive, which refer to the situation when the theory derives hypothesized relations between economic variables that are not known or have not been identified by research but can be confronted by empirical evidence. At best these theories only explain the known facts and represent the concept in a more fashionable way. This is a degenerating program in Lakatos's description. This assessment of internalization is made with a basic assumption that we are all in the positivist economic paradigm, otherwise there are always alternative views on the research methodology issues.

Another major criticism is on the empirical deficiency of internalization. There is voluminous literature that claims to provide evidence in support of the theory. These studies, however, fail to establish an empirical design to falsify the theory, and their conclusions are doubtful. With the predominance of internalization and industrial organization, a meaningful approach to differentiating these theories should be to test competing hypotheses derived from them. Suppose there are competing theories, X and Y. The test of the theory would require us to formulate hypotheses that are discriminative—that is, they should be the predictions of distinctive observations that can be derived from either theory X or Y, but not both. Based on the evidence, the theory can be confronted, and we may claim that the study results either support or reject a theory. The degree of testability will increase if these two theories provide predictions of opposite outcomes. Based on the results, we would conclude either theory X or Y. On the other hand, if these two theories provide predictions agreeable to each other, the test then is inconsequential and meaningless. We should have saved ourselves the trouble of testing.

That is the kind of problem that can be found in the empirical literature of internalization. The major approach is based on the examination of relationships between the level of foreign involvement and various firm-specific measures, such as spending on research and development (R&D) and on advertising, and the ratio of engineers to total employment. These variables are used as major proxies for the firm's intangible assets in the internalization approach. However, they also have a conceptual link to the industrial organization literature and are accepted as measures of entry barriers and market power (Bain 1956, Lall and Siddharthan 1982, Muller and Tilton 1969). Consequently, confirmation of the relationships does not differentiate the internalization hypothesis since they can also be explained in the industrial organization framework. In fact, these relationships have been investigated in prior industrial organization literature. For the same reason, the firm's internal exports relative to R&D cannot be an effective measure of internalization (Buckley and Brooke 1992). The market-value-based study does not rectify the problem either. Morch and Yeung (1991) found a positive relationship between the firm's value measured by Tobin's q ratio and its levels of R&D and advertising spending, and this relation becomes more significant for the firm with a higher level of foreign involvement. They concluded that the firm's internalization enhances the value of its intangible assets and thus supports the internalization theory. However, the same evidence can also be interpreted in the industrial organization framework. That theory suggests that the firm's foreign investment enhances its market power and ability to earn monopoly rent. As such, the value creation associated with FDI should be greater for firms with greater market power (measured by the R&D and advertising proxies). That is the rationale used for a similar empirical design and evidence interpretation in the prior industrial organization study.[3] Even a more sophisticated event study (Morch and Yeung 1992) cannot be claimed as the test of the internalization theory. That study found that firms with higher levels of R&D spending have experienced more positive abnormal returns at FDI announcements. The authors concluded that the evidence supports the internalization theory, suggesting that FDI by know-how-intensive firms is more profitable and thus enhances the value of intangible assets. However, it may be premature to conclude that the valuation effect represents the present value of increased foreign earnings in the future. As Errunza and Senbet (1981) contended, in an efficient capital market, the advantage of the MNE should have been fully incorporated into the stock price, which explains why the stocks of the MNE and the domestic firm provide the same risk-adjusted returns. If their argument is correct, then this valuation effect may represent the information conveyed by the act of FDI announcements. In short, empirical researchers fail to establish a setting to differentiate the internalization theory, and the validity of their studies thus can be questioned.

In comparison, industrial organization research has an apparent advantage over internalization research in terms of empiricalness. The former provides more convincing evidence in support of the market power hypothesis. Although it generates some empirical implications that are undistinguishable from those of internalization, there are findings that belong exclusively to the industrial organization framework. Such findings include the pattern of oligopolistic response in the firm's FDI behavior, the relationships between foreign investment and the market power measured by the Herfindahl Index and the four-firm or eight-firm concentration ratio, and so on. The strength of industrial organization research is that it is based on a theoretical framework with higher empirical content. This branch of economics started with a strong empirical tradition. It was originally developed due to an antitrust concern and sought to assess the social and economic consequences of corporate expansion. As a result, this research develops a framework that can more easily generate empirically testable hypotheses. When this framework is applied to explain the multinational enterprise, the theory is endowed with high empirical content. This is a luxury which the internalization theory does not have. Given the low empirical content of the internalization framework, it is difficult to transform the theory into an empirical format and subject it to a test.

The empirical limitation of internalization has been recognized by many authors on different occasions, and it is the underlying reason for Kay's criticism (1983) that internalization is not a theory. Although we do not select a theory based purely on empirical contestability, a research paradigm can be considered scientific or acceptable only if it has empirical implications. Indeed, the imperative task of internalization research should be to enhance the empiricalness of the theory. That should be the current direction of internalization research.

SUMMARY

We conclude the review with some critical comments on the internalization theory. The major point is that the internalization theory in the course of its development has shown the pattern of a degenerating program. However, our intention is not to deny the merits of this theory but to challenge readers to think more critically about some fundamental philosophical and methodological issues of research. Obviously, it is easy to criticize, but a criticism without constructive suggestions will not be meaningful to future research. Furthermore, the empirical deficiency of internalization is something that has already been recognized by internalization scholars. What really matters is how to rectify the problem and direct the research to progressive problemshifts.

Here we can further see the power of Lakatosian guidelines. While recognizing that a research program will be eliminated if it produces long-term degenerating shifts and if a better alternative is available, Lakatos (1970) also suggested that a research program may experience a temporary degenerating phase. Then the invention of new auxiliary hypotheses and discovery of new facts will again lead to progressive problemshifts. For such a direction, Lakatosian approach further provides guidance to research, holding that researchers should seek progressive problemshifts by pursuing positive heuristic (namely, refutable hypotheses) and avoiding negative heuristic (namely, irrefutable hypotheses).

Lakatos's paradigm has a direct relevance to research on the MNE and its foreign investment: The progressiveness of internalization research lies in the development of auxiliary hypotheses and in devising "conjectures which have more empirical content than their predecessors" (p. 132). This is also consistent with Buckley's suggestion (1988) of formulating some special theory. Overall, Lakatos's views provide great insights and signify the importance of FDI signaling research. First, the FDI signaling proposition is testable empirically. Furthermore, it is derived from the internalization theory. Consequently, it represents an auxiliary hypothesis which not only provides additional explanation but also enhances the empirical content of internalization. It is a research of progressive problemshifts in Lakatos's sense.

NOTES

1. It is a relatively more recent issue for Americans to experience the anxiety of foreign ownership of domestic corporate assets. The United States, with its increasing inflows of foreign capital, has become the single largest recipient of foreign direct investment. This triggers public concern and even a fear of foreign control, which led to the current regulatory moves discriminatory against foreign-owned companies (e.g., Theofilopoulou 1989).

2. This point can be exemplified by the wage difference between foreign-owned companies and American-owned companies in the United States. Foreign companies are found to pay higher wages than American companies in all sectors of the economy. In 1991, for example, the average pay at a foreign-owned company was $42,431, while the average pay at an U.S.-owned company was $38,002. See the U.S. Bureau of Economic Analysis, *Foreign Direct Investment in the U.S.: Operations of U.S. Affiliates* (Washington, D.C.: U.S. Department of Commerce, 1996).

3. As if in support to such an argument, Tobin's q ratio is considered a measure of monopoly rents in the industrial organization approach (Lindenberg and Ross 1981, Salinger 1981). Hirschey (1982a) and Kim and Lyn (1986) conduct market-value-based studies to investigate the cause of foreign direct investment and generate the results similar to Morch and Yeung's study (1991). The interpretation, however is made in the industrial organization framework.

4

The Signaling Framework
of Foreign Direct Investment

The internalization paradigm is criticized for a lack of dynamics in explaining the process of a firm's multinationalization (Teece 1985). As a result, it fails to provide a framework with which to examine the behavioral interactions between international oligopolies (Vernon 1985). This criticism in fact has identified a major weakness of the theory—it rationalizes foreign direct investment with external and internal variables as fixed and given. The MNE thus is assumed to pursue foreign investment as a maximization strategy without considering its market consequences. This approach is static because it neglects the possible reaction of other firms and the MNE's behavioral modification in anticipation of this reaction. In response to Vernon's criticism, Dunning (1988) acknowledged the existence of such interactions but argued that it was beyond the scope of the neoclassical model to consider these effects. This defense is not convincing. Since the theory is built on the premise of imperfect competition, it should be logical for us to expect the MNE's action to draw certain market reactions and to consider the implications of these reactions. The evidence presented by Knickerbocker (1973) showed that the FDI action exhibits the pattern of oligopolistic response, with one firm's foreign entry triggering similar actions by its major competitors in a highly concentrated industry. To explore the interactions in the internalization framework, we need to extend the theoretical basis of internalization, which will be the task of this chapter.

While the industrial organization framework considers mainly the interactions between competing firms at a horizontal level, we further postulate that certain interrelations exist between the firm and other market participants, including buyers, suppliers, and investors. In a real world with uncertainty, when these outsiders do not have full information about the firm's capabilities and intentions, their perceptions and thus their behavior would be influenced by the firm's FDI behavior. However, if FDI is a calculated move of the investing firm, as is commonly believed, these subsequent effects should be foreseen by the firm before taking the action. In anticipation of these effects, the firm will then modify its subsequent investment behavior. In other words, in a world of imperfect information, there are actions and reactions among the MNE and other market participants. These interactions are examined in this chapter. Specifically, we are interested in the effects of these interactions on the MNE's investment behavior and the competitive equilibrium established in the market in light of these effects. Our discussion starts with a review of the market signaling literature, and it is followed by development of the FDI signaling framework, which provides a conceptual basis on which to examine foreign direct investment in an interactive market setting. In this setting, we can explore the perceptual impact of the investment and assess the interactions in the MNE's external markets.

THE MARKET SOLUTION TO INFORMATION IMPERFECTION

The thesis of internalization theory is that foreign direct investment is an economic solution to transactional market imperfections. In other words, when information asymmetry makes it costly to use the market for transactions, the firm opts to bypass the market and internalize know-how products. This is the major justification of foreign direct investment provided by internalization theory. However, an issue of concern is how transactions are organized by multinationals in markets with imperfect information. This issue is relevant not only because market transactions still represent a major part of an MNE's international activities but also because the economists believe that the market has the inherent mechanism to correct such market imperfection. The latter point can be understood after we have a review of literature in information economics.

The behavior pattern in the imperfect information situation is a major consideration on which internalization is rationalized. However, the asymmetric structure of information exists not only in the market for know-how but also in many other markets, in different forms, and to varied degrees. For example, a used-car buyer may not be fully informed by the seller about the true state of the car, an employer is unlikely to be fully aware of a job applicant's productivity, a person seeking legal services normally does not have adequate knowledge to judge lawyers' professional qualifications, and an investor does not have the same information as a manager regarding a firm's earning prospects. In all these cases, information asymmetry exists because transaction parties cannot effectively communicate with each other. The opportunistic nature of human behavior is a major obstacle. For example, when the quality of a product is unobservable, a producer of good quality has an incentive to tell the market about its quality, but a producer of poor quality will make the same (false) claim about its quality. Talk is cheap when it is not verifiable, and verbal communication is ineffective in conveying the message. As a result, the buyer cannot determine the quality of products before purchasing, and there is great uncertainty associated with market transactions.

Akerlof (1970) examined the outcome of imperfect information or the "lemon problem" in the used-car market. Obviously, quality varies among used cars. While the seller normally knows more than the buyer about the quality of the car, an information asymmetry exists in the market. When quality is unobservable, the market can only price all cars according to the average of quality. At that price, however, the seller of highest quality is not adequately compensated and hence may decide to withdraw from the market. Consequently, the price of remaining products in the market will be reduced to reflect the new average of quality, and this will lead to the withdrawal of the seller with the second highest quality from the market. This process will continue until all the next-best products have left the market. At the end, only products of lowest quality remain in the market; Thus, a product being in the market is self-evidence of a lemon. The important conclusion of this analysis is that in situations of imperfect information about quality, the bad products (lemons) may drive good products out of the market.

Market failure, however, is not generally observed in reality. For example, Bond's study (1983) failed to detect the existence of "the lemon problem" in the used-truck market. The integrity of the market is preserved because the market will develop some mechanisms to counteract the uncertainty associated with asymmetric information. One such mechanism is the brand name. When buyers cannot perfectly determine quality before consumption, they make decisions in repeated purchases based on prior experience. Thus when a firm intends to stay in the market for a significantly long time, it seeks to establish reputation by pursuing quality consistence. Presumably, the information asymmetry is more severe in the market for consumer goods and services, and thus more brand names have been developed in these sectors. For example, Hilton, Hyatt, and Holiday Inn in the hotel business and McDonald's, Burger King, and Subway in the fast-food business are all well-known names. Given its role to reduce buyer uncertainty, the brand name also has a market value. Thus, PepsiCo was willing to pay a premium price to acquire the name products such as Kentucky Fried Chicken, Pizza Hut, Frito-Lay, and Taco Bell.

Another mechanism to counteract buyer uncertainty is product warranty, which is a promise made by the seller to allow returns if the product is perceived unsatisfactory. The warranty essentially transfers buyer uncertainty from the buyer to the seller. It also works as a signal. There is a cost associated with the product warranty, since the producer has to bear the cost of returned products. The producer is willing to make this promise because it gains additional sales. Competitors, to maintain their market share, must follow suit. The warranty, however, is not like some business practices that can be easily duplicated by all other producers. The cost of the warranty varies across firms and is higher for firms with lower quality, with a higher return rate associated with lower quality. Assume each producer knows its own quality, the low-quality producer will choose not to provide a warranty, if its expected cost is higher than gains from offering a warranty. Since the firm's decision whether to offer a warranty is based completely on self-interest, this act becomes a credible signal. It provides buyers a cue to differentiate firms of varied quality in the market.

This discussion introduces the basic concept of a market signal, which refers to an observable action or attribute adopted by a firm or an individual which, by design or accident, conveys information to less informed market participants. A rigorous signaling model was first developed by Spence (1973, 1974) in the context of the labor market. First, a worker's contribution to production is measured by marginal labor productivity, which varies among individuals. If the individual ability is known in the market, then each will be paid according to his or her marginal labor productivity. However, labor productivity is an unobservable attribute, and thus each job applicant is more aware of his or her own ability than is a potential employer. When an employer cannot determine the productivity of individuals in the job market, it can only set a uniform wage based on the average productivity of all workers. As a result, the more productive individuals will be under-paid, and the less productive individuals will be over-paid. This motivates the under-paid individuals to acquire a certain observable attribute—a signal—that will differentiate them in the market. Thus, a differential wage scale can be established. However, if such a signal exists, then all individuals, including those less productive ones, should have an obvious interest in acquiring the signal. As such the signal cannot be credible. For example, formal dress in a job interview is highly recommended by experts. However, if this dress could project a professional image, then each job applicant will buy (or even borrow) an elegant suit for the event, and the job interviewer is unable to use this indicator to differentiate job applicants in the market. Obviously, a signal can be effective only if it is difficult, or even impossible, for less productive individuals to imitate it. Consequently, Spence (1972) concluded that a signal can be credible only if the acquiring cost is negatively associated with the unobservable feature that it intends to reveal. In the labor-productivity case, when the additional cost for less productive individuals to acquire the signal is greater than the gain derived from the signaling, it would be in their interest *not* to mimic the signal. As a result, an employer can differentiate job applicants of varied productivity.

Figure 4.1
Individuals' Productivity and Education Choices

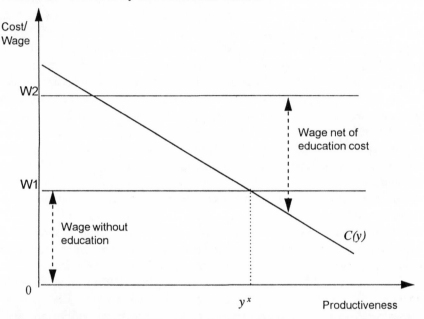

In Spence's study (1973), the education index is considered a market signal. The analysis starts with the cost of education, which is in a broad sense and includes elements such as the length of time, financial resources, and mental efforts required for an individual to finish his or her education. Assume that the education cost is negatively associated with labor productivity (we may think that there is a common factor, say, intelligence, affecting these two variables in the opposite way; that is, an intelligent person is more productive and can finish his or her education with lower cost). Then an education-based wage scale can be developed, which will lead to individualized education choices, which in turn enables employers to differentiate individuals of different productivity levels. A simplified version is presented in Figure 4.1. The horizontal axis measures individuals' productive levels (y), and the vertical axis measures levels of education cost and wage (measured by the net present value of all future incomes from employment).

The education cost function $C(y)$ is a downward slope, indicating that more productive individuals are expected to incur less costs to acquire education. While each individual's productivity is unobservable, the employer sets a wage scale at two levels: a wage of W2 for those with education above a certain level, say, a bachelor's degree, and a wage of W1 for those without the degree. A person's payoff then is equal to the wage net of the education cost. When individuals make choices to maximize their respective payoffs, they will choose either not to acquire any education and receive a payoff equal to W1, or acquire an education (but no more than a bachelor degree) and receive a payoff equal to W2 minus their education costs. As shown in the figure, individuals with a productivity level at y^x are indifferent to the choice on education. However, individuals with productivity less that y^x will be better off not acquiring any education and individuals with productivity above y^x will be better off getting a bachelor's degree. In other words, self selection will take place, and individuals will make choices based on their inherent productivity. Then they can be differentiated based on the unobservable attribute of productivity—a person's choice to acquire an education is an indication that his or her productivity is y^x or above. The education signal is credible because individuals' choices are guided by their self-interest.

In summary, the signaling mechanism develops in markets with imperfect information. With the signal conveying information to less informed market participants, the uncertainty associated with market transaction is reduced. A major consequence of signaling, therefore, is that it may improve the information structure and allocative efficiency of the market. After Spence, Rothschild and Stiglitz (1976) independently developed a similar signaling model in the insurance market. Riley (1979) further established the general conditions for a signaling equilibrium with mathematical rigor. Since then, the signaling paradigm has been widely applied in research. Studies suggest that various firm actions are credible signals used by management to convey information about the aspects of the firm known to the market, including product warranties (Grossman 1981, Spence 1977), capital structure (Ross 1977), entrepreneurial ownership retention (Leland and Pyle 1977), dividend announcement (Miller and Rock 1985), direct accounting disclosure (Hughes 1986), the choice of auditors (Balvers et al. 1988), general financial decisions (Talmor 1981), and advertising (Ippolito 1990).

FDI SIGNALING: ITS RATIONALIZATION

So far we have presented two alternative approaches to coping with market imperfections. The internalization literature focuses on replacement of the market, suggesting that foreign direct investment be a vehicle by which the firm internalizes transactions and bypasses the market. On the other hand, information economics suggests that the market develop a self-correcting mechanism to cope with market deficiencies. One such mechanism in particular is the market signal, which corrects information asymmetries and facilitates market transactions. The second approach is interesting because it implies that the existence of market imperfections does not necessarily lead to the breakdown of the market. It is relevant to the study of the MNE because this economic institution is still actively involved in the market part of international know-how transfer despite the known hazards in the market.

In the last two decades the international market for know-how has experienced substantial growth. Today an MNE is more likely to transfer know-how by various market and quasi-market arrangements such as turnkey projects, licensing, management contracts, and joint ventures. The literature justifies the MNE's willingness for externalization by various considerations, such as the host government's restriction on foreign control, the gains from strategic alliances with other major firms, the individual firm's resource constraints, and the MNE's preference to commercialize the less proprietary technology (e.g., UNCTC 1988). All these explanations can be easily integrated into the framework of transaction cost economics, which provides a dichotomy on transactions that will be organized in the market and that will be internalized. Despite these justifications, given the MNE's active role in the external market, an important question still can be raised: What is the market consequence of the MNE's foreign investment?

The industrial organization literature raises this issue in the market structure context and extensively examines the market consequence of foreign investment. In contrast, internalization theory rarely considers the consequence of FDI in the transactional market context. Of course, this would not be an issue had the MNE's internalization replaced its market transactions completely. However, since the external market continues to be a significant part of the MNE's international resource transfer, we must ask (1) what is the consequential effect of the firm's FDI internalization on transactional market imperfections (2) will the firm's FDI internalization affect the market part of its transactions? While turning the focus of analysis to market transactions, we pay particular attention to the MNE's approaches to manage transactions in the market with imperfections and determine whether the MNE engages in any activity to overcome information imperfection in the market. These issues are derived from the internalization framework but are largely neglected by the literature.

Casson (1982) dealt with these issues when he extended the internalization theory to explain multinational enterprises in some low-tech industries.

He suggested that there is great buyer uncertainty in the markets for services and consumer products, because consumers generally lack information about quality. When quality control becomes an overriding consideration, sellers may integrate backward to production across national borders. While this strategy ensures quality consistence, the multinational firm represents brand names that build up consumer confidence. The consumer's identification of brand-name products helps overcome buyer uncertainty. This approach not only explains prevalence of multinationals in hotels, fast-food restaurants and consumer products, but also represents a radical departure from the internalization in a conventional sense, which focuses on foreign investment mainly as a substitute for the market. When Casson argued that the multinational is established to maintain reputation and reduces buyer uncertainty, the justification of direct investment is based on recognition of the effect on the MNE's market transactions. He essentially argues that, with the MNE's engagement of foreign investment, transactional market imperfections are reduced. This has become the main thesis of this book, which considers FDI as a mechanism for correcting information imperfection and facilitating the multinational's transactions in the marketplace.

The market consequence of internalization can be further established in the FDI signaling framework, which recognizes the perceptual effect of foreign investment and explores its implications in the MNE's external market. We start with a brief summary of the consequential effect of FDI in Figure 4.2. The analysis starts in box 1, which is based on the postulation by Hymer (1976), Dunning (1979, 1981) and others that the multinational enterprise is characterized by firm-specific advantages based on know-how intangible assets. In the absence of transactional market imperfections, the firm would exploit these assets by market transactions. The existence of market imperfections such as information asymmetry, however, gives rise to market failure, which inspires the firm to pursue FDI internalization. As indicated by the flow directed to box 2, the firm undertakes direct investment to transfer know-how within the organization and exploit the benefits of know-how itself. Because of the additional costs associated with foreign production, as shown in box 2a, the firm's FDI action may also be a cue to less-informed outsiders, indicating that the firm's know-how advantage is at least superior enough to offset its disadvantage operating in a foreign market. This leads to the major proposition of this book that the firm's FDI action has perceptual effects on outside investors and buyers, which is expressed by the flow from box 2 and 2a to box 3. As such the FDI action results in a flow of information in the market, as shown by the flow from box 3 to box 4. This information flow reduces the asymmetric information structure and subsequently promotes the firm's transactions in the market, and this connotation is shown by the connection between box 1 to box 4. By and large the MNE's foreign investment may promote its markets for know-how-based intermediate and finished products. Therefore, a conceptual link can be established between the MNE's internalization and external market operations under the FDI signaling framework.

The center of analysis is that a firm's FDI action may alter the perceptions and beliefs of other market participants with less information. While inside information is generally unavailable to these outsiders, the firm's action of internalization may reveal certain information to them. This point can be illustrated by an extension of Akerlof's analysis on the used-car market. Let us consider a negotiation between the seller and buyer of a used car. The buyer is likely to be less knowledgeable than is the seller about the true state of the car. Suppose that, in response to the buyer's offer, the seller claims that the car is worth more than the offered price and even declares: "with that price I would keep the car for myself." This assertion may be true or may be a bluff, but the buyer cannot be sure because he does not have all the information to verify the seller's claim. However, upon the seller's action to withdraw from the market (assume this withdrawal is irreversible and he cannot come back to the market again), the claim becomes credible. In this case, the very action of the seller choosing self-use may alter the perception of the buyer, telling him that the car is worth more than the offered price or what is perceived in the market. When an action carries a message and changes the perception, it is said to have information content.

Figure 4.2
The Consequential FDI Internalization

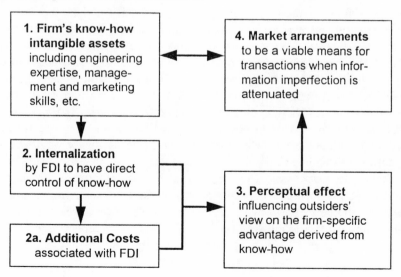

This analogy can be applied to the rationalization of foreign direct investment. The firm's FDI action reflects its preference for self-use to market transfer of know-how. This preference may further affect outsiders' perceptions. These less-informed market participants, while not having full access to information about a firm, will take a cue from certain actions adopted by the firm. This point can be seen more clearly through the following analysis. Assume that the firm's management pursues profit maximization (or maximization of the present value of the firm's cash-flow streams). Thus it will prefer internalization to externalization if its know-how intangible assets are correctly priced in the market. On the other hand, internalization will be preferred if its intangible assets are under-valued by the market. An example would be that a firm chooses foreign production if it cannot obtain acceptable terms from licensing of know-how. However, management's action to choose FDI also reflects its belief that internalization can bring a greater value to the firm. Obviously, management's choice and belief are based on an overall assessment with a particular consideration on the nature of its know-how advantage and the additional cost associated with foreign production. Furthermore, this assessment is based on all information at hand, including the inside information. Although this information may not be available to outsiders, it in effect has been revealed to them by management's choice of FDI internalization. Upon seeing the FDI move, these market participants will make an inference, correctly, that the firm's intangible assets should be more valuable than what is perceived in the market. In other words, the firm's FDI action results in conveying information to the less-informed market participants, who consequently will modify their perceptions about the firm's know-how intangible assets.

In the preceding two examples, although similar perceptual impacts are suggested for the used-car seller's choice of self-use and the MNE's internalization, there is a major difference in results. Whereas the former represents a seller's withdrawal from the market, internalization only changes the form of the firm's products transacted through the market. FDI internalization means that, instead of selling know-how intermediate products, the firm sells finished products embodying know-how. In addition, it may pursue an FDI strategy to serve one country market but a licensing strategy to serve another market, or use an FDI strategy for one type of production and licensing for another type. Finally, no matter what foreign expansion strategies are pursued, management has to consider the consequences in the stock market, that is, their effects on the prices of the firm's stocks. The main point is that internalization does not disconnect the firm from the markets. However, if the firm only internalizes part of its markets, and if this internalization alters the market perception, the market consequence of this perceptual effect should be an issue deserving our attentions. In the connotation of FDI signaling effects, these issues are thoroughly explored in this chapter.

We postulate that the FDI action may alter the market perception of the firm's know-how intangible assets, attenuate market imperfections, and promote its market transactions. However, the Spence-type signaling equilibrium further requires that the cost to acquire such a signal be negatively related to the know-how attribute, which would deter the firms of inferior know-how from mimicking the signal. Otherwise these firms would all have an incentive to imitate the signal (that is, to take some foreign investment and join the club of multinationals) and misinform the market of its know-how capacity. If that happens, the signal is false and can no longer effectively differentiate firms in the market. In the FDI signaling paradigm, this signaling condition is satisfied by the cost nature of foreign production. The Hymer-Kindleberger paradigm rationalizes FDI with recognition of the additional cost of foreign production—because of the firm-specific advantage, FDI is a rational choice despite the inefficiency associated with the operations in a foreign territory. This concludes that the firm-specific advantage is a necessary condition for FDI—namely, only the firm in possession of such an advantage may have an interest in foreign investment. Without this advantage, a firm is not competitive overseas and thus unwilling to take the risk. This implies self-selection—the firm that pursues foreign direct investment is the one that has the firm-specific advantage at least superior enough to offset the additional cost of FDI. In other words, a firm's engagement in foreign production is self-evidence of its possession of firm-specific advantage. This gives rise to the FDI signaling role: Based on the nature of foreign production costs, FDI becomes a credible signal conveying information about its know-how intangible assets. However, FDI should be more relevant to the firms in the industries whose major firm-specific advantage is derived from know-how intangible assets, which are proprietary in nature and thus cannot be adequately valued by the market.[1]

The FDI signaling postulation is further illustrated in Figure 4.3. The cost and revenue of foreign production are measured by the vertical axis, while the levels of foreign production and firm-specific know-how are measured along the horizontal axes to the right and left, respectively, of the vertical axis. TC_A, TC_B, and TC_C each represent the cost functions of firms A, B, and C. With the given revenue function TR, it is not profitable for firm A to undertake FDI and hence the firm will not do it. Firms B and C will undertake foreign investment to their optimal levels at Y_B and Y_C, where the marginal revenues equal the marginal costs, and incur foreign production costs C_B and C_C, respectively. The variation of foreign production costs among firms is caused by difference in their know-how levels, which is the relation expressed by the contour to the left of the vertical axis. A downward slope indicates that a firm with a higher level of know-how has a lower production cost. With firm B's know-how, the profit from foreign operations is zero. Therefore, K_C is a cutoff point, and those firms with know-how within the range of 0 and K_C will remain domestic. While these firms' managers make choices based on their respective know-how levels, the true state of the firm-specific know-how is assumed to be incompletely known to the market. We further assume that the effect of know-how on the firm's production costs is known to the public. Consequently, when outside market participants have only incomplete information about the firm's know-how capability but can observe the firm's FDI posture, they will make inferences on the firm's relative know-how position based on the observed foreign production level. As the implications reflected in Figure 4.3 show, the firm should have firm-specific know-how at least above a certain level before it becomes involved in foreign production. Moreover, the firm with a higher level of know-how should have more extensive foreign involvement, as suggested by Dunning (1973). Therefore, in a market with asymmetric information about know-how quality, a firm's FDI reveals the true state of its know-how to the market and thus has information content.

Figure 4.3
Firm's Know-How and Related FDI Levels

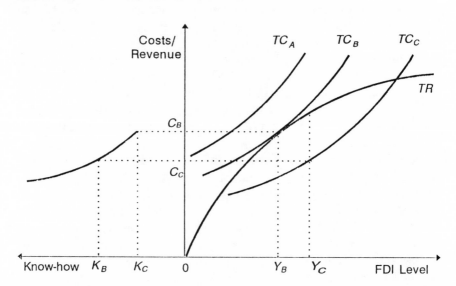

The preceding scenario shows that firms with different know-how levels have different optimal levels of foreign production. In reality, the foreign investment environment varies across countries, which affects the level of additional cost associated with foreign production. This additional cost is the lowest for the countries with the most favorable investment environment and is the highest for the countries with the most undesirable environment. Each firm, given its level of firm-specific know-how, will then make a choice in foreign expansion. It will start progressively, from the most desirable foreign market to the next desirable one, and finally will come to a level at which the additional gains match the additional costs. This suggests that the more superior a firm's know-how advantage is, the more extensive its foreign involvement will be in the process of the firm's expansion. In summary, there is a positive association between the level of know-how and the multinationality of the firm, and such a relationship thus ensures the separating equilibrium.

SUMMARY

A firm's possession of superior know-how gives it the incentive and capability to become a multinational enterprise. The firm probably undertakes foreign direct investment with internalization as its original purpose and seeks to bypass the market with asymmetric information. This action, however, may have an additional consequence—it conveys information to less-informed outsiders and tells them something about the quality of the firm's know-how intangible assets. As a result, the firm's FDI action becomes a market signal which influences perceptions of these market participants. The existence of this signaling effect may give the firm an additional incentive to pursue the path of multinationalization of the firm. Exploration of these implications requires us to develop a Spence-type signaling model in a more rigorous fashion and to satisfy the basic conditions for a signaling equilibrium. This will be the task of Chapter 5.

One critical point should be mentioned before the conclusion of this chapter. The FDI signaling proposition is derived with an emphasis on knowledge-based intangible assets and failure of the know-how market. However, three types of FDI have been identified in the literature— horizontal, vertical, and international diversification—and failure of the know-how market is considered mainly an explanation for the horizontal foreign investment (Caves 1982, Teece 1981b). While FDI signaling is derived from the market failure framework, it is most relevant to the horizontal MNE. In other words, FDI signaling effects are most likely to be observed among knowledge-intensive firms and in the industries where the know-how advantage is the utmost determinant of competition. This consideration further directs us to develop an empirical design to differentiate the FDI signaling effects from other effects of foreign direct investment.

NOTE

1. Superior knowledge is a major form of firm-specific advantage, but the firm-specific advantages can also be in some other forms, such as economies of scale, control of sources of cheap raw materials and supplies, and access to the world market. However, only when the primary source of a firm's advantage is knowledge-based, information imperfection then becomes a major driving force for the firm's FDI internalization, and FDI signaling plays the role. This situation provides us with a systematic way to empirically differentiate the signaling effect from other effects of foreign direct investment, as shown in chapters 6 and 7.

5

Modeling the FDI Signaling Effects

In this chapter, we construct some simple models with which to explore the signaling implications of an MNE's foreign investment. While this exploration is based on assumptions, postulates, and theories developed in the mainstream FDI literature, it not only helps us understand the inherent relationships of various economic variables but also generates propositions with empirical implications. Consequently, the FDI signaling theory can be tested. The model development consists of three parts. First we present a basic model of foreign production in the internalization framework. Next from the model we generate the results which provide a direction to explore the interrelations of the firm's internalization and externalization in a multinational setting. Afterwards, the valuation of the firm is examined in the FDI signaling framework. Finally, the chapter will be concluded with a summary of major results generated from signaling modeling.

THE BASIC MODEL OF FOREIGN PRODUCTION

The basic model of internalization is developed by incorporating the major literature on FDI and the MNE. The discussion starts with a firm before it becomes a multinational. The firm thus operates in the home country, and its profit in any single period can be expressed as

$$\Pi_d = PY_d - C_d(Y_d, K, L_d) + \varepsilon, \qquad (5.1)$$

where Π is the profit; P is the product price; Y is the output volume and a measure of the production level; K is the firm-specific know-how; L is the country-specific location factor; C is the general production cost function determined by Y, K, L; ε is a random error with the expected value $E(\varepsilon) =$

0; and the subscript d denotes the firm's domestic operations.

The location factor L synthesizes the effects of environmental variables on production costs. It has been recognized that business costs are directly affected by location-specific variables, such as the price of inputs, labor costs and productivity, infrastructure development, government policy and taxes, and cultural context. The location factor may not be a consequential consideration in a cross-sectional study of firms operating in a domestic setting because it affects all firms in the same fashion. However, it is important to explain foreign production in the paradigm of imperfect competition. The variation of location factors across countries influences the direction of FDI flows because firms seek the least cost location for production (Caves 1982, Dunning 1973, Hirsch 1976, Kojima 1978).

The firm's production cost is affected by its level of production and know-how in the following manner:

$$C_Y > 0, \quad C_{YY} > 0; \quad C_K < 0, \quad C_{KK} > 0, \quad C_{YK} < 0. \tag{5.2}$$

These conditions are defined by the law of the diminishing rate of return. The effect of output level on the cost is reflected in the conditions for C_Y and C_{YY}. Furthermore, we assume that the major benefits from know-how superiority is the cost advantage.[1] Thus a firm's production cost is also affected by the type of know-how employed in the operation. The inequality $C_K < 0$ indicates that an increase in the level of firm-specific know-how leads to a decrease in overall costs, and $C_{KK} > 0$ further suggests that the marginal impact of know-how application on cost reduction diminishes with the increasing level of the firm-specific know-how. Furthermore, although an increase in the output level leads to an increase in cost (given $C_Y > 0$), this cost increment should be smaller for a firm with a higher level of know-how (i.e., $C_{YK} < 0$). A more detailed discussion on decreasing marginal returns from know-how application is presented by Magee (1977).

The firm is further assumed to have a know-how advantage. To reap the benefits of multiplant economies of scale associated with know-how, the firm seeks to exploit the know-how in the foreign market. Licensing appears to be the first choice, given the additional cost incurred by a firm undertaking foreign production. Under the licensing agreement, the firm can transfer its know-how to a native firm in the foreign country, and, in return, it will have a time stream of revenues in the form of licensing fees. However, given imperfect information as well as other market imperfections, know-how cannot be correctly priced. As such, licensing becomes less appealing to the know-how owner. The firm prefers self-use to maximize its returns from ownership of know-how. Consequently, it establishes foreign production and becomes a multinational and competes with native firms there. This MNE's foreign profit function then is

$$\Pi_f = P(Y_f, Y_n) Y_f - C(Y_f, K, L_f) - C2(Y_f) + \varepsilon, \qquad (5.3)$$

where the subscript f denotes the variables of the firm's foreign operations and n denotes the variables of a native firm in the foreign country; P is the price determined by Y_f and Y_n, the output level of the firm and native firm in the foreign country; and C is the production cost determined by Y_f, K, and L_f. Notice that the same notation K is used for the MNE's domestic and foreign operations, indicating that know-how is firm specific and can be transferred within the firm internationally. Furthermore, the firm also incurs $C2$, the additional cost of foreign production, as a result of its unfamiliarity with foreign environments and discriminatory practices of the host government. This cost is assumed to satisfy

$$C2_Y > 0, \qquad C2_{YY} > 0. \qquad (5.4)$$

After the firm is multinationalized, it competes directly with the native firm in the foreign country, whose profit function is

$$\Pi_n = P_n(Y_n, Y_f) Y_n - C(Y_n, k, L_f) + \varepsilon, \qquad (5.5)$$

where subscript n denotes the variables of the native firm, and the lowercase k is used to represent the know-how of native firms and distinguish it from K, the MNE's know-how.

With two firms in consideration, the setting represents an oligopolistic market structure. Here the firms sell similar, but not perfect substitute, products.[2] Thus the price for each firm's products is determined not only by its output level but also that of the other firm. Each firm assumes the other's output is fixed, and chooses a profit-maximizing output level accordingly. Market equilibrium is established through the interaction of firms. The Cournot-Nash equilibrium yields the optimal production levels Y_f^* and Y_n^* that satisfy

$$\Pi_f' = P(Y_f^*, Y_n^*) + \frac{\partial P(Y_f^*, Y_n^*)}{\partial Y_f} Y_f^* - \left. \frac{\partial C(Y_f^{*\prime} K)}{\partial Y_f} \right|_K - \frac{\partial C2(Y_f^*)}{\partial Y_f} = 0, \qquad (5.6)$$

$$\Pi_n' = P_n(Y_n^*, Y_f^*) + \frac{\partial P_n(Y_n^*, Y_f^*)}{\partial Y_n} Y_n^* - \left. \frac{\partial c(Y_n^{*\prime} k)}{\partial Y_n} \right|_k = 0. \qquad (5.7)$$

In this situation, if the firm earns negative profits, it will eventually leave the industry. And if it makes economic profits, this invites new entries to the industry and competition will drive down the profits. Consequently, the firm in the long run makes a zero profit. That is,

$$\Pi' = PY_f^* - C(Y_f^*, K, L_f) - C2(Y_f^*) = P_n Y_n^* - C(Y_n^*, k, L_f) = 0. \qquad (5.8)$$

Given the additional cost $C2$ incurred by the MNE and the condition $C_K < 0$ in equation (5.2), $K > k$ is implied. In other words, only the firm with know-how superior enough to offset its disadvantages from producing abroad will undertake foreign production. Equation (5.8) thus serves as a self-selection criterion. With the know-how level and production cost function different among firms, a separating equilibrium exists. This is critical to ensure that the FDI action is a credible signal.

Since each firm seeks to maximize its profit by producing at a level where the marginal revenue equals the marginal cost, the observed production levels of the MNE and native firm are assumed to be the optimal Y_f^* and Y_n^* in equations (5.6) and (5.7). Given this situation, only K, k and L_f are unknown variables, which then can be determined by jointly solving equations (5.6), (5.7), and (5.8). In other words, the level of firm-specific know-how K can be derived, and this implicitly defines it as a function of Y_f; that is, $K^* = K^*(Y_f)$. This inverse function represents an important conclusion: FDI provides the outsider with a basis to make an inference about some unobservable feature of firm, and by undertaking FDI, the firm has in effect revealed its true know-how to the market with asymmetric information. The implications will be further examined in the next two sections.

SIGNALING EFFECTS IN THE MNE'S PRODUCT MARKETS

A typical MNE, besides internalizing, is also actively engaged in market transactions to transfer its intermediate assets and finished products across countries. The neoclassical approach in general assumes that the MNE seeks an optimal level of FDI, but rarely considers the effect of this action on its operations in the external market. However, we have shown that this FDI action reveals the nature of the firm-specific know-how and thus affects the market perception. Therefore, an FDI signaling model can be developed to explore the cross effects of the firm's FDI on its transactions in the markets of intermediate and final products. The following discussion starts with the MNE's external market transactions, or its externalization.

Let X represent the MNE's profit from its external market transactions, which is suggested to be positively associated with the firm's know-how K.

As Buckley and Casson (1976) suggested, the firm's sales are a result of the market demand, which ultimately is determined by the quality of its know-how. However, we have already recognized that, in the market with asymmetric information, this know-how is not fully known to outsiders. When the buyer does not have full information, his or her view and behavior are based on the perception of firm-specific know-how. Therefore, the market demand, and hence the firm's profit X, is rather an outcome of market perception denoted $\tilde{K}$. More specifically, the MNE's profit function of externalization is $X(\tilde{K})$, with a relation such that

$$\frac{dX}{d\tilde{K}} > 0. \qquad (5.9)$$

With imperfect information about know-how in the market, the buyer's perception of a firm's know-how will be affected by certain actions taken by the firm. In forming his or her perception of the firm's know-how, the buyer utilizes the information revealed by its FDI, or the K^* estimation derived from the observed Y_f^* and Y_n^* in equations (5.6), (5.7), and (5.8), and the other relevant information Z. Consequently, the inference schedule is

$$\tilde{K} = \theta K^*(Y_f) + (1-\theta)Z = \tilde{K}(Y_f), \qquad (5.10)$$

where θ is the weight that the buyer assigns to the signal in estimating the value of know-how.

Substituting equation (5.10) into X, the MNE's profit from externalization, the function then can be further expressed as $X(\tilde{K}(Y_f))$. This function implies that the MNE's profit of externalization is associated with the market perception of the firm's know-how, which, in turn, is influenced by the firm's FDI level.

Furthermore, the MNE is assumed to optimize the aggregate profits from its foreign involvements, including both internalization and externalization activities, thus:

$$\max_{Y_f} \Pi = PY_f - C(Y_f, K, L_f) - C2(Y_f) + X(\tilde{K}(Y_f)). \qquad (5.11)$$

Equation (5.11) captures the essence of the FDI signaling model: The firm's choice of FDI not only determines its profits from foreign production, but also affects its profits from external market transactions. This is because the firm's FDI choice affects the buyer perception of its know-how, which in turn influences the market demand for its know-how-associated products, which will influence the overall performance of the firm.

Equation (5.11) represents the first condition required for a signaling equilibrium: The MNE chooses an FDI scale (a signaling level), with consideration of its impact on buyers' perceptions of the firm's know-how, to maximize its given objective function. The second required condition is that the market correctly identifies the MNE's know-how:

$$\tilde{K} = K. \tag{5.12}$$

This suggests that the buyer's perceptions of a firm's know-how agree with the firm's true know-how. Otherwise the signal is false, and the market will not reach an equilibrium. As proved by Riley (1979), both conditions (5.11) and (5.12) must be satisfied simultaneously for the signaling equilibrium.

Propositions

We have just presented the FDI internalization and signaling models, which provide rich implications for the explanation of FDI patterns. Some propositions are demonstrated and explained as follows.

Proposition 1: The value of the same know-how product varies to the foreign firms across countries.

PROOF: The maximum value of know-how to the foreign user can be measured by the additional cost offset by the MNE's know-how advantage, $C2(Y_f^*)$, which is determined by the country-specific Y_f, L_f, and $\partial C2/\partial Y_f$. Therefore, the value of the know-how is also country specific.   □

This may explain why the MNE often prefers to license rather than sell know-how to foreign firms. With a licensing arrangement, the MNE's royalty and licensing fees, while being determined by negotiation, are based on the sales volume and negotiation and are country specific.

Proposition 2: The firm's foreign production expansion positively affects its market transactions, i.e., $dX/dY_f > 0$.

PROOF: According to equations (5.9) and (5.10),

$$\frac{dX}{dY_f} = \frac{dX}{d\tilde{K}}\theta\frac{dK^*}{dY_f}. \tag{5.13}$$

Let

$$f(Y_f, K) = P + \frac{\partial P}{\partial Y_f}Y_f - \frac{\partial C}{\partial Y_f} - \frac{\partial C2}{\partial Y_f}, \tag{5.14}$$

where

$$\frac{\partial f}{\partial K} = -\frac{\partial^2 C}{\partial Y_f \partial K} > 0,$$

$$\frac{\partial f}{\partial Y_f} = 2\frac{\partial P}{\partial Y_f} + \frac{\partial^2 P}{\partial Y_f^2}Y_f - \frac{\partial^2 C}{\partial Y_f^2} - \frac{\partial^2 C2}{\partial Y_f^2} < 0.$$

(5.15)

Since $f(Y, K^*) = 0$, differentiating both sides, we have

$$\frac{\partial f}{\partial K^*}dK^* + \frac{\partial f}{\partial Y_f}dY_f = 0, \qquad (5.16)$$

$$\frac{dK^*}{dY_f} = -\frac{\partial f/\partial Y_f}{\partial f/\partial K} > 0. \qquad (5.17)$$

Because $dX/d\tilde{K} > 0$ by assumption, $dX/dY_f > 0$. □

With information revealed by FDI signaling, the firm's foreign production may affect the market perception of the firm's know-how. This results in outward shifting of the demand curve for the firm's products and expansion of its transactions in the external market.

Proposition 3: The existence of FDI signaling motivates the firm to expand its foreign production more aggressively, to a level beyond the optimal point prescribed by the internalization model; that is $Y_s^* > Y_I^*$.

PROOF: Since Y_I^* is the solution to

$$f(Y_f, K) = P + \frac{\partial P}{\partial Y_f}Y_f - \frac{\partial C}{\partial Y_f} - \frac{\partial C2}{\partial Y_f} = 0, \qquad (5.18)$$

$$f(Y_I^*, K) = 0.$$

Let Y_s^* be the solution to

$$g(Y_f, K) = P + \frac{\partial P}{\partial Y_f}Y_f - \frac{\partial C}{\partial Y_f} - \frac{\partial C2}{\partial Y_f} + \frac{dX}{dY_f} = 0, \qquad (5.19)$$

$$g(Y_s^*, K) = 0.$$

According to Proposition 1, $dX/dY_f > 0$; thus

$$f(Y_p,K) < g(Y_p,K). \qquad\qquad (5.20)$$

Then

$$f(Y_S^*,K) < g(Y_S^*,K) = f(Y_I^*,K) = 0. \qquad\qquad (5.21)$$

Since $\partial f/\partial Y_f < 0$, therefore $Y_S^* > Y_I^*$.   □

Figure 5.1
Different Perspectives of FDI Optimization

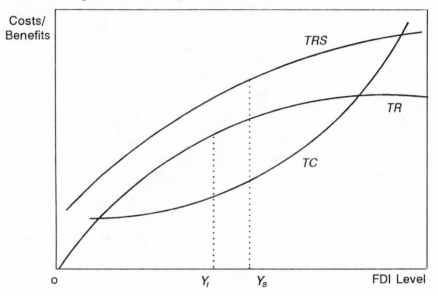

Note: $TR = PY$, total revenues from a firm's foreign production;
      $TRS = PY + S$, total FDI revenues plus FDI signaling Gain;
      $TC = C + C2$, the firm's total foreign production costs.

As illustrated in Figure 5.1, the optimal FDI level derived from the internalization model is at Y_I^*, where the marginal revenue is equal to the marginal cost and the firm maximizes its profit from foreign production. However, the recognition of FDI signaling benefits will motivate the firm to invest to the level at Y_S^* to maximize the total benefits of FDI operations. A neoclassical economist will consider a firm's FDI at this level as overinvested abroad, because the firm's operating profit from foreign production is less than that at Y_I^* level. The reduction of foreign profit as a result of expanding FDI from level Y_I^* to level Y_S^* is the signaling cost and represents "a welfare loss in comparison to the would-be foreign production level in absence of market imperfections, which is the (unattainable) symmetric information equilibrium" (Strong and Walker 1987, p. 148).

Figure 5.2
Returns on Assets for Firms Operating in the United States

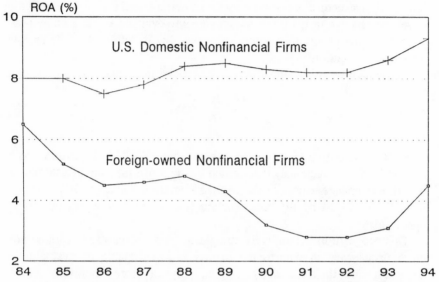

Source: U.S. Department of Commerce, Bureau of Economic Analysis, *Current Survey of Business* (1996), Federal Reserve Board, *Balance Sheets for the U.S. Economy 1945-94.*

Stated in nontechnical terms, the preceding argument means that when the MNE status is perceived as a reputation, the firm will be more aggressive in pursuing multinationalization of its operations, even to a level beyond that justifiable by the profit maximization stand. The neoclassic economist would consider that level of FDI as overinvested abroad. It has been noticed (McClain 1983) that the average rate of return on equity for the U.S. affiliates of foreign multinationals is 3 to 4 percentage points lower than the average of all nonpetroleum industries in the 1975–80 period. An examination based on more comprehensive data further yields support for the findings (see Figure 5.2). Although the difference in the rate of returns is subject to different interpretations, it is consistent with the FDI signaling proposition, which suggests the optimal level of foreign production is calculated with a consideration on the signaling gain associated with FDI.

Proposition 4: The effect of a firm's FDI to promote its external market is positively associated with the proprietary nature of firm-specific know-how.

Know-how is a stock of proprietary knowledge. It, by nature, is an indivisible commodity (that is, the market value of know-how is zero if all other firms can have the same access to the know-how). As a result, the firm has a strong incentive to preserve the proprietary nature of its know-how. Thus the larger the size of the stock, the more asymmetric the information structure is associated with its market, and the more heavily the buyer may have to rely on the market signal to evaluate a firm's know-how. Therefore, the proprietary nature of know-how is reflected in the relative weight θ in equation (5.10).

Consequently, this proposition can be proved mathematically by showing

$$\frac{\partial}{\partial\theta}(d\frac{dX}{dY_f}) > 0. \tag{5.22}$$

PROOF: Equation (5.13) clearly shows that dX/dY_f is proportional to θ, since $dX/d\tilde{K}$ is exogenously determined by the profit function of externalization (the exchange aspect of the MNE's operations) and dK^*/dY_f is exogenously determined by the cost function (the production aspect of MNE's operations). $\qquad\square$

This proposition is intuitively straightforward. With a firm's know-how more proprietary in nature, the market is less capable of evaluating it correctly, and thus the market signal plays a more important role in influencing the buyer's decision. Consequently, a firm's FDI has more substantial effects in promoting its transactions in the external market.

Proposition 5: The firm's level of foreign production is positively associated with the proprietary nature of its know-how, that is $dY_f^* /d\theta > 0$.

PROOF: Y_f^* is the solution to

$$g(Y_f^*,K) = f(Y_f^*,K) + \frac{dX}{d\tilde{K}}\theta\frac{dK^*}{dY_f}\bigg|_{Y_f^*} = 0. \tag{5.23}$$

Differentiate both sides:

$$\frac{\partial g}{\partial Y_f^*}dY_f^* + \frac{\partial g}{\partial\theta}d\theta = 0. \tag{5.24}$$

Therefore,

$$\frac{dY_f^*}{d\theta} = -\frac{\partial g / \partial \theta}{\partial g / \partial Y_f^*}. \tag{5.25}$$

Since

$$\frac{\partial g}{\partial \theta} = \frac{dX}{d\tilde{K}} \frac{dK^*}{dY_f}, \tag{5.26}$$

and given the conditions in equations (5.9), (5.17), and (5.19),

$$\frac{dX}{d\tilde{K}} > 0, \quad \frac{dK^*}{dY_f^*} > 0, \quad \frac{\partial g}{\partial Y_f^*} < 0. \tag{5.27}$$

Therefore,

$$\frac{dY_f^*}{d\theta} > 0. \qquad \square$$

This suggests that the firm with know-how that is more proprietary in nature tend to undertake foreign production more extensively. With such a relationship, the multinationality of the firm provides an indication for know-how superiority. This proposition is supported by the fact that MNEs generally concentrate in know-how-intensive, high-skill industries with higher spending on R&D and advertising, which have been justified by the existing literature. Industrial organization theory approaches the issue in the context of market power, and internalization theory suggests that the transactional market is more imperfect for know-how products, which gives the firm a stronger incentive to bypass the market. Based on the signaling paradigm, there is another explanation: The firm is more driven to signal its know-how quality to the market and overcome information imperfection in the market.

Finally, the signaling mechanism of foreign investment can be briefly summarized by Figure 5.3. The vertical axis on the left is the know-how index, the horizontal axis measures the foreign production level, and the vertical index on the right represents the effect of FDI on the firm's external market transactions. The relationship between the know-how index and foreign production indicates that a firm must have the firm-specific know-how at least at the level of K_M before it becomes a multinational. Furthermore, the firm with a higher level of know-how will be more extensively involved in FDI. This relationship establishes the MNE status as a reputation for know-how superiority. A positive association is further reflected in the FDI axis and the market-effect axis. Because of the FDI signaling effect, a higher level of FDI will promote the firm's external market transactions to a greater extent. The integration of the whole diagram suggests that a firm with a higher level of know-how should have the FDI action affecting its market transactions to a greater extent.

Figure 5.3
The Market Consequence of FDI Signaling

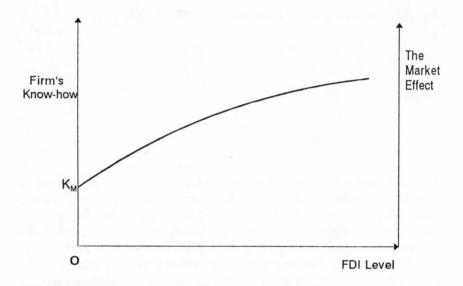

FDI SIGNALING AND VALUATION EFFECTS

The preceding section considered the market consequence of FDI signaling mainly in the product markets. The signaling proposition, however, further has its implications for the financial market. The finance literature has recognized that asymmetric information exists in the financial market, between the inside managers and outside investors, on the potential payoff and thus the value of the firm's assets (Miller and Rock 1985, Myers and Majluf 1984, Ross 1977). This research, however, has not explicitly identified sources of information imperfection. This line of research can be extended with recognition of internalization theory, which suggests that one type of information asymmetry is associated with the market evaluation of the firm's know-how intangible assets. In other words, if FDI signaling truly conveys information about the firm's know-how intangibles, it should have relevance to the market valuation of the firm as well. Consequently, a firm's FDI action may affect the value of the firm. The implications of FDI signaling can be explored through modeling the valuation process of the multinational firm.

Valuation Under Symmetric Information

The analysis starts with the first stage of the firm, when it has only domestic operations. Assume that outside investors and inside managers have the same access to the information about the firm, including those factors which affect the firm's current and future earnings. Given the profit maximization function in equation (5.8), the value of the firm equals the present value of future earnings plus the cash in hand. For simplicity, we further assume that the firm has zero growth for its domestic profits. The value of the firm in the first stage thus can be expressed as

$$V_1 = \int_{t=0}^{\infty} \Pi_d^* e^{-rt} dt + A = \frac{\Pi_d^*}{r_d} + A, \qquad (5.28)$$

where V_1 denotes the value of the domestic firm, A is the total cash in the firm, and r is the risk-adjusted rate of return. In the second stage of the firm's development, when it expands overseas by undertaking FDI with its available funds, the value of the firm can be expressed as

$$V_2 = \frac{\Pi_d^*}{r_d} + \frac{\Pi_f^*}{r_f}, \qquad (5.29)$$

where V_2 denotes the value of the firm in the second stage, after foreign expansion, and is equal to the sum of the present values of future domestic and foreign earnings Π_d^* and Π_f^*, which are defined in equations (5.1) and (5.3). The implication based on the Modigliani and Miller theorem (1958) is

$$A = \frac{\Pi_f^*}{r_f}, \quad and \quad V_1 = V_2. \qquad (5.30)$$

In other words, in the perfect market with symmetric information, the firm's decision whether to undertake FDI is irrelevant to its market valuation.

Valuation Under Asymmetric Information

In reality, however, there is asymmetric information in the market, and outsiders do not have all information about the firm-specific know-how K and thus are not fully aware of the true profits and costs of the firm. However, we assume that the market knows that the firm's know-how is in a range between K_L and K_H, where

$$K_L < K < K_H. \tag{5.31}$$

When the market does not have full information about the firm specific know-how, it can price it only according to $\bar{K}$, the market average. From this average, the market value of the firm can be derived. Consequently, the value of the firm can be rewritten as

$$\bar{V}_1 = \frac{\Pi_d(\bar{K}, Y_d^*)}{r_d} + A. \tag{5.32}$$

Based on the profit function in equation (5.1) and condition $C_K < 0$ in equation (5.2), the firm with $K > \bar{K}$ has a true value greater than the market average (that is, $V_1 > \bar{V}_1$). This suggests that the firm with superior know-how will be underpriced in the market. The difference between the true firm value and the market estimation, $\Delta V_1 = V_1 - \bar{V}_1$, stems from the firm's know-how superiority and is defined as the value of intangible assets.

When the firm is undervalued in the market, it has a strong incentive to reveal its true know-how level and correct the information asymmetry. As a result, FDI signaling arises. The analysis in the first section of this chapter concludes that, based on the firm's FDI internalization, outsiders can make a correct inference on the true state of its know-how. In other words, the firm's FDI action may affect the market valuation of know-how intangible assets. Given the FDI effect on the market perception of know-how, the firm's know-how is defined as an implied function of FDI; that is, $\tilde{K} = \tilde{K}(Y_f)$ (see the discussion on p. 84). Consequently, the term reflecting the MNE's domestic assets can be expressed as

$$\tilde{V}_d = \frac{\Pi_d(Y_d, \tilde{K}(Y_f))}{r_d}. \tag{5.33}$$

Therefore, the MNE valuation model in equation (5.29) can be rewritten as

$$\max_{Y_f} V_2 = \frac{\Pi_d(Y_d, \tilde{K}(Y_f))}{r_d} + \frac{\Pi_f(Y_f, K)}{r_f}. \tag{5.34}$$

Equation (5.34) represents the first condition required for a signaling equilibrium: The MNE chooses an FDI scale (a signaling level), considering its perceptual impact on the market, to maximize its given objective function.

The second condition required for an equilibrium is that the market correctly identifies the MNE's know-how, as reflected in equation (5.12). Both conditions in equations (5.34) and (5.12) must be satisfied simultaneously for the signaling equilibrium.

Propositions

Based on the FDI signaling valuation model, we can identify some inherent relationships among FDI, firm-specific know-how, and the firm's value. This provides conceptual guidance for developing an empirical framework with which to examine the FDI signaling theory.

Proposition 6a: The firm's FDI expansion positively affects the value of the firm.

Proposition 6b: The FDI valuation effect represents a revaluation of the firm's domestic assets.

Propositions may be proven by showing that $\partial \Pi_d / \partial Y_f > 0$.

PROOF: According to equation (5.33),

$$\frac{\partial \Pi_d}{\partial Y_f} = \frac{d\Pi_d}{dK} \frac{dK}{dY_f}. \tag{5.35}$$

From Proposition 5, $dK/dY_f > 0$, and

$$\frac{d\Pi_d}{dK} = -\frac{dC_d}{dK} > 0. \tag{5.36}$$

Therefore, $\partial \Pi_d / \partial Y_f > 0$. $\square$

The FDI signal conveys to the market the information about the firm-specific know-how. As a result, a firm's FDI may change the market perception of the firm and result in revaluation of its intangible assets. Proposition 6b suggests that this value appreciation is not derived from the firm's future FDI earnings, and thus differentiates the FDI information content from the valuation effect possibly associated with the operational gain of foreign production.

Proposition 7:   *The valuation impact of FDI signaling is positively associated with the proprietary nature of the firm's know-how.*

Under asymmetric information, the market can estimate individual firms' know-how quality only according to the market average. As a result, when a firm's know-how is more proprietary in nature, the discrepancy between the true know-how and the market average is greater in magnitude. Thus the proprietary nature of know-how can be estimated by the difference between the market's posterior inference of know-how $\tilde{K}(Y_f)$ and its prior estimation $\bar{K}$; that is, $\Delta K = \tilde{K}(Y_f) - \bar{K}$. Furthermore, the valuation effect of FDI can be measured by the difference between the domestic asset value inferred from FDI and that estimated without FDI, i.e., $\Delta V_d = \tilde{V}_d - \bar{V}_d$. Therefore, the proposition can be proven by showing that $\Delta V_d/\Delta K > 0$.

PROOF: Based on equations (5.1), (5.2), and (5.33), it is clear that

$$\frac{\partial V_d}{\partial K} = \frac{1}{r_d}\frac{d\Pi_d}{dC_d}\frac{dC_d}{dK} > 0. \tag{5.37}$$

Therefore, ΔV_d is positively associated with ΔK.   □

This proposition is intuitively straightforward. If the valuation effect of FDI is truly attributed to FDI signaling, it should be more substantial for the firm whose intangible assets represent a larger portion of total value. Since the assets of these firms are priced under more imperfect information, a greater value correction should result upon information conveyed by FDI signaling. Based on this proposition, the FDI signaling effect is differentiated from the valuation effect associated with diversification and tax arbitrage gains.

The propositions derived from the FDI signaling model specify certain interrelations among FDI, firm-specific know-how, and the value of the firm. While these postulated relationships can be confronted by evidence, the modeling provides conceptual guidance for an empirical investigation of FDI signaling theory. The empirical studies of FDI signaling theory will be conducted in Chapter 6 and Chapter 7.

NOTES

1. A firm's know-how advantage may result in various benefits, such as development of new products, reduction of costs, increase of output, and improvement of quality (UNCTC 1988). However, all these benefits in essence can be categorized into the creation of two types of competitive advantages: product differentiation or cost advantage (Porter 1980). For simplicity, we follow Arrow (1971) and consider cost reduction as the major benefit derived from know-how application. Thus the firm with superior know-how has a lower level of production cost. Alternatively, we may assume that product differentiation is the major benefit derived from know-how advantage. In that case, the effect of firm-specific know-how will be reflected in the difference in prices, and this effect can then be shown by the expression of $P_f(K)$ and $P_n(k)$. This change, however, will not alter the results generated from the modeling.

2. For simplicity, we consider the case in which there are only two firms, the MNE and the native firm, in the market. The analysis, however, can be further extended to that with multiple firms and thus representing monopolistic competition. For more on various forms of competition, see Varian (1984).

6

Evidence of Relationships Between the MNE's Internalization and Externalization

The literature has identified two types of market signals: One is a specific action adopted by the firm, and the other is the preannouncement of an action made by the firm (Heil and Robertson 1991, Porter 1980). To examine the signaling effect of foreign direct investment in these two contexts, therefore, we organize the empirical investigation into two parts. The purpose of this chapter is to determine the consequence of the MNE's investment action in its "real" product markets, based on the statistical relationships between the firm's FDI internalization and its market transactions of licensing and direct exports. Chapter 7 examines the financial market reaction to the preannouncement of the MNE's foreign investment, by measuring the firm's stock price adjustment at its FDI announcements. The propositions generated in Chapter 5 help us construct an empirical framework with which to test the signaling theory.

HYPOTHESES AND PRIOR LITERATURE

To investigate the interrelations between the MNE's internalization and external market transactions, we must develop an empirical classification of transaction types and proxy measures of different variables. According to Buckley (1989), the MNE's international involvements can be empirically measured by *TFR*, the total foreign revenues, and

$$TFR = FSS + LCS + XPT, \tag{6.1}$$

which suggests that the MNE's international involvements consist of three major components: *FSS* is the sales of the firm's foreign subsidiaries and a measure of the level of its FDI internalization, *LCS* is its licensing revenues from unaffiliated foreign firms, and *XPT* is its direct exports to foreign markets. The latter two measure the MNE's market transactions of know-how products and finished products, respectively. Notice that each component is the summation of a specific type of transaction that consists of a range of products serving a number of foreign countries.

If there are no interaction effects between different components, the MNE will adopt a piecemeal approach to each foreign entry, assessing benefits and costs associated with alternative entry modes and choosing one that can bring the maximum net-of-costs gain. The firm's foreign involvements as a whole also will be optimized. This is the traditional approach based on the transaction cost paradigm. However, if interaction effects exist between different transactions, such effects will be part of consideration in the firm's foreign expansion decision. The FDI signaling proposition suggests that the MNE's foreign investment promote its market transactions of intermediate and finished products. As such, the MNE, in assessing an FDI opportunity, will not only consider its operational costs and benefits but also its effects on market transactions. Therefore, the MNE will adopt an integral approach to its various forms of foreign involvements rather than seek separate optimization, and it will pursue maximization of its total profits from foreign involvements.

Hypothesis Construction

The interrelations among different types of an MNE's international involvements are thoroughly explored through model development in Chapter 5. Proposition 2 suggests that an MNE's internalization have positive effects on its external market transactions, and this can be transformed to empirically testable hypotheses as follows:

Hypothesis H1a: *An MNE's licensing revenues from unaffiliated foreigners are positively associated with its foreign subsidiary sales, ceteris paribus.*

Hypothesis H2a: *An MNE's direct exports to foreign markets are positively associated with its foreign subsidiary sales, ceteris paribus.*

In the context of equation (6.1), these hypotheses suggest that the firm's expansion of *FSS* will lead to the growth of *LCS* and *XPT*. The firm's FDI may promote its market because this action alters the market perception and then induces the demand for the firm's products. Therefore, the FDI

signaling theory predicts that a firm's foreign production will be complementary to its external market transactions.

In search of global optimization, the MNE may choose different
strategies for different products and different strategies to serve different
country markets.   The proposed complementary relationships of FDI
signaling are based mainly on the cross-product and cross-market effects of
the MNE's foreign expansion. The argument can be more clearly presented
by Figure 6.1. For simplicity, we consider a case in which an MNE is in a
business consisting of three products—namely, *P-I, P-II,* and *P-III*—and
serves three foreign markets, countries A, B, and C.   The firm may
undertake foreign production of product *P-I* in country A, while licensing
the production of *P-II* and directly exporting *P-III* to the same market.
Meanwhile, it may directly export product *P-I* to country C and license the
know-how of *P-I* to country B.   Given the perceptual effect of FDI
(indicated by the broken line in Figure 6.1), the MNE's foreign production
of *P-I* in country A may promote the licensing of *P-II* and direct export of
P-III to the same country, and promote the direct export and licensing of *P-I*
to countries C and B.   Therefore, the firm's FDI overall may be complementary to its exports and licensing.

Figure 6.1
FDI Effects on an MNE's Market Transactions

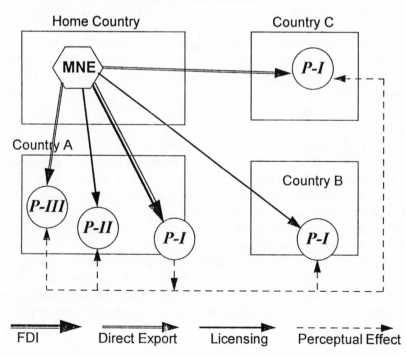

A FDI signaling test, however, is misspecified if it is based entirely on confirmation of a market response to the signaling event (Acharya 1988). In other words, even if a positive relationship is found between the MNE's internalization and externalization (or a firm's stock price increases at its FDI announcement in Chapter 7), it may be due to reasons other than FDI signaling. For instance, a firm's foreign production of one product may create market demand for its associated products and thus promote the firm's direct exports of these products to that country market (or a firm's FDI is expected to improve its earnings prospects, and thus the FDI announcement may have a value effect). Therefore, the confirmation of H1a and H2a still does not provide exclusive support to FDI signaling. Furthermore, the test based on these hypotheses is ineffective in identifying the market response with the presence of both complementary and substitute effects. Such substitute effects may exist. For example, the internalization theory considers FDI mainly as a substitute for exports and licensing, for it internalizes transactions that otherwise will take place in the market.[1] This indicates that the observed relationship between the firm's foreign production and market transactions is only the net of these complicated effects.

Given this complexity, the tests of hypotheses H1a and H2a can no longer effectively separate the FDI signaling effect from other operational effects. If the study finds a positive and significant correlation between MNEs' internalization and externalization, this relationship can be due to FDI signaling but may also be caused by some unidentified exogenous variables that affect these two types of activities concurrently. An acceptance of the FDI signaling proposition may lead to a Type I error, an incorrect rejection of the null hypothesis. Alternatively, if the signaling effect exists but is dominated by the substitution effect of internalization, a negative relationship will be found between the firm's foreign production and exports/licensing. This test would lead to a rejection of the FDI signaling proposition and thus commit a Type II error. Therefore, since hypotheses H1a and H2a are unable to differentiate various effects of foreign production, an FDI signaling test based on these hypotheses is inadequate.

One solution is to disaggregate the firms' data of foreign production, exports, and licensing by geographic regions and product lines. The signaling test can be performed by examining the cross-product and cross-region effects of FDI on exports and licensing. Such disaggregated data, however, is publicly unavailable, and the test is largely impossible. An alternative approach to the test is based on Proposition 4, which suggests that the positive relation between FDI and market transactions, if it is explained by FDI signaling, should be more significant for firms with more proprietary know-how. This implication can be transformed into empirical hypotheses as follows:

> *Hypothesis H1b:* *The positive relationship between foreign subsid-*
> *iary sales and licensing revenue from unaffiliated*
> *foreigners is greater for an MNE with a higher*
> *level of know-how intensity, ceteris paribus.*

> *Hypothesis H2b:* *The positive relationship between foreign subsid-*
> *iary sales and direct export is greater for an MNE*
> *with a higher level of know-how intensity, ceteris*
> *paribus.*

The intuition underlying these two hypotheses is quite simple. According to the FDI signaling paradigm, the role of FDI signaling arises mainly as a result of information-related imperfections in the market for know-how. If a firm's production is based on a higher level of know-how intensity, its markets should present more asymmetric information. Thus, the buyer has more difficulty in evaluating the products, and his or her perception is more likely to be affected by the firm's signaling action. Consequently, FDI signaling plays a greater role in conveying information in the market for more sophisticated know-how. As such, hypotheses H1b and H2b postulate that, should the relationship between FDI and the market transactions be explained by FDI signaling, this relationship would be greater in magnitude for firms with more intensive know-how. These two hypotheses provide a primary basis for the signaling test because they differentiate the FDI signaling effects from other operational effects of foreign production.

Prior Empirical Research

There is a large body of empirical literature on MNEs' operations, which is guided mainly by the industrial organization and internalization frameworks. This literature produces rich evidence on the interrelations between various forms of the firms' foreign involvements. However, few studies provide results that can be used to evaluate the implications of FDI signaling. One possible explanation is that such effects do not exist. More likely, however, it is because research has largely neglected the signaling issue and thus fails to develop a theoretical framework to explore these interrelations. The latter point becomes more clear after a brief review of existing empirical literature.

Whether foreign direct investment is a substitute for or complementary to international trade has been subject to a historical debate (see Hood and Young 1979, Musgrave 1975). At the economy level, FDI can be trade-generating because it may lead to additional demand from the foreign subsidiaries for the products of the parent or other companies in the home country. However, if the output by foreign subsidiaries replaces exports from the parent or its other affiliates, then FDI substitutes for trade. The nature of the relationship between FDI and trade has been intensively investigated by prior research. Applying some simple statistical analysis, Gruber et al. (1967) found exports to be positively associated with R&D and foreign production. Other studies examined various other issues such as the relationship between multinationals' trade and foreign investment (Helleiner 1973, Morley and Smith 1971, Riedel 1975), the determinants of intrafirm trade (Cho 1990, Lall 1981, Helleiner and Lavergne 1979) and the effects of FDI on exports (Horst 1972b, Lipsey and Weiss 1981). However, these studies employed the industry-aggregate data, and the interpretation of results at the firm level is rather restricted.

A firm-level study was done by Lipsey and Weiss (1984). While they measured exports alternatively by the firm's total exports or the intrafirm exports, the results indicated that U.S. firms' foreign production may positively affect their exports to a given foreign region. The findings are consistent with the internalization theory, which suggests that internal markets created by FDI facilitate flows of goods and services within the firms. The interfirm exports were not specifically considered in that study. Furthermore, the relationship between MNEs' foreign production and exports is a complicated matter. For example, a recent study by Anderson and Fredriksson (1996) based on Swedish MNEs suggested that the foreign affiliates of MNEs have a tendency to export more if the parent companies are less involved in foreign production and in the industries with lower levels of R&D spending.

The relationship between FDI and licensing sales has also been studied in different contexts. Based on a survey of some U.S. multinational firms, Telesio (1979) found that the firms more actively engaged in licensing are likely to be those which (1) spend more on R&D, (2) are more diversified, (3) are relatively small in their industries, and (4) have less experience in foreign operations. His study suggests that licensing complements foreign production for those firms. On the other hand, Contractor's study (1985), based on data aggregated at the industry level, found a negative association between FDI and licensing, suggesting a substitute relationship between these two modes of international know-how transfer. Contractor, however, did not pay attention to the effect of know-how intensity, that is, whether the relationship between FDI and licensing varies systematically across firms of different know-how intensity. This is an issue that is crucial to the FDI signaling theory but not addressed by other research.

The empirical evidence on the relationship between FDI and external market transactions is limited, mainly due to two reasons. First, there is a lack of publicly available data. For example, firms' licensing revenues are generally not disclosed to the public. Second, the theoretical research fails to provide conceptual guidance on these relationships (Lipsey and Weiss 1984), although a complementary relationship between internalization and market transactions is postulated by Williamson (1975). The internalization framework, in explaining the firm's choice between FDI and alternative modes of foreign involvements, provides a clear direction on the relationship between a firm's FDI and internal market transactions. However, it lacks implications on the link between internalization and externalization.[2]

RELATIONSHIPS BETWEEN FDI AND LICENSING

Based on the FDI signaling proposition, the MNE's foreign investment position promotes its transactions of know-how in the international market. Empirically, it suggests that the level of *FSS*, the MNE's foreign subsidiary sales, should be positively associated with the level of *LCS*, its licensing revenues from unaffiliated foreign firms, in equation (6.1). The interrelations between these two variables are further specified by hypotheses H1a and H1b, which are to be tested by multiple regression analysis.

Specification of the Empirical Model

In the context of Hypothesis H1a, we develop a basic empirical model as follows:

$$LCS_{lt} = \lambda_0 + \lambda_{1l}FSS_{lt} + \lambda_2 TSL_{lt} + \lambda_3 Ind_{lt} + \lambda_4 Yr_t + \mu_{lt}, \qquad (6.2)$$

where LCS_l is the licensing sales to unaffiliated foreigners by MNEs in industry l, FSS_l is the foreign subsidiary sales of MNEs in industry l, and TSL_l is the total sales of MNEs in industry l; these variables are deflated by MNEs' domestic sales to correct cross-sectional heteroskedasticity. In addition, *Ind* is a dummy variable to control for the industry effect and equal to 0 for manufacturing and 1 for nonmanufacturing industries, and *Yr* is the dummy variable to control for the variation resulting from changes of various external variables across periods and equal to 0 for year 1977 and 1 for 1982.

Hypothesis H1a proposes a positive relationship between an MNE's *FSS* and its *LCS*, and thus predicts the λ_1 coefficient to be positively significant. Hypothesis H2b further postulates that the relationship between *FSS* and *LCS* is greater in magnitude for firms with higher levels of know-how intensity. Empirically, this suggests that the λ_1 coefficient vary cross-sectionally and is greater for MNEs with higher levels of R&D spending. This relation is expressed as

$$\lambda_{1l} = \chi_0 + \chi_1 KH_l, \tag{6.3}$$

where KH_l is the industry level of know-how intensity estimated by R&D spending as a percentage of sales. We can substitute equation (3) into (2) to yield a full model:

$$LCS_{lt} = \lambda_0 + \chi_0 FSS_{lt} + \chi_1 KH \cdot FSS_{lt} + \lambda_2 TSL_{lt} + \lambda_3 Ind_{lt} + \lambda_4 Yr_t + \mu_{lt}. \tag{6.4}$$

Equations (6.3) and (6.4) should generate similar results on the coefficient estimation. However, only the full model in equation (6.4) will be examined in this chapter since it provides more degrees of freedom and thus leads to less estimation error. Hypotheses H1a and H1b suggest that χ_0 and χ_1 both be positive. However, if the substitution effect of internalization exists, it is possible to find a negative χ_0 coefficient. Therefore, the validity of the FDI signaling proposition critically depends on the t-statistics of χ_1, which is explicitly to be positive, as the signaling role is more relevant to firms whose competitiveness is based mainly on know-how intangibles and thus in the markets presenting more information imperfection.

Sample and Measurement of Variables

The primary sources of data are surveys published by the U.S. Department of Commerce. Under the International Investment Survey Act of 1976, the Bureau of Economic Analysis (BEA) undertakes a benchmark survey on U.S. foreign direct investment activity approximately every five years. This study obtains data from the survey results published in *U.S. Direct Investment Abroad 1977,* which includes 3,540 U.S. multinational firms and their 24,666 foreign subsidiaries, and *U.S. Direct Investment Abroad: 1982 Benchmark Survey Data,* which includes 2,245 U.S. multinational firms and their 18,399 foreign subsidiaries. These surveys cover all major aspects of U.S. multinationals and provide the most comprehensive statistics on U.S. firms' foreign operations. To ensure confidentiality, the data are aggregated at the three-digit level of the BEA industry classification code. Furthermore, the data are suppressed for industries that consist of only a small number of firms to avoid revealing specifics of individual firms.

The sample includes 143 observations from 73 industries based on the three-digit BEA industry code in the years 1977 and 1982. However, there are missing values in the data. Some observations are suppressed by BEA for confidentiality, and others are replaced with a sign when the value is $500,000 or less. Thus total observations for the all-foreign-subsidiary group and majority-owned group are 112 and 111 for the basic model and 98 and 95 for the full model. The data items collected for this study are as follows: U.S. parent firms' receipts of royalties and licensing fees, parent firms' total sales, total exports, R&D expenditures, exports to foreign affiliates and to unaffiliated foreigners, and foreign-subsidiaries' total sales.

The dependent variable LCS_i, measured by the parent's receipts of royalties and licensing fees from unaffiliated foreigners, is a proxy for the MNE's know-how transactions in the external market. Based on BEA's definition, royalties and license fees include fees and other receipts from the use or sale of intangible assets or intellectual property rights, such as patents, industrial processes, trademarks, copyrights, franchises, designs, formulas, techniques, and manufacturing rights.

The independent variable FSS_i is a proxy for the size of foreign production and equals the foreign subsidiaries' total sales minus their purchases from parent firms. The variable TSL_i equals the parents' sales plus subsidiaries' sales minus the intrafirm transactions, and it is to control the variation of dependent variables attributed to size. Variable KH_i, the proxy for know-how, is calculated by dividing R&D expenditures by the parent's total sales.

Results and Interpretation

Table 6.1 reports the estimated regression coefficients and their t-statistics for licensing transaction models. The first column lists the independent variables included in the empirical models. The second and fourth columns report the results from applying the basic model of equation (6.2) to the data of all foreign subsidiaries and majority-owned foreign subsidiaries. The λ_2 coefficient on TSL is significantly greater than zero, suggesting that firms with higher levels of total sales receive higher levels of licensing revenues. Thus, the variation of licensing revenues across firms is partially explained by the size effect. With λ_3 coefficient on Ind being negatively significant, the firms in the manufacturing industries generally have higher levels of licensing revenues. This suggests that firms in these industries either are more involved in a licensing strategy for international know-how transfer or have know-how advantages (such as engineering techniques) in a form more ready for market transfer. Finally, the λ_1 coefficients on FSS are found to be negative and significant. Therefore, on average, firms with more active involvement in foreign production are likely to receive less licensing revenues. The results reject hypothesis H1a and conclude that FDI may be a substitute for licensing

The regression results for the full empirical model based on equation (6.4) are further presented in the third and fifth columns of Table 6.1. The

Table 6.1

Relationships Between MNEs' Licensing Sales and Foreign Investment

$$LCS_{lt} = \lambda_0 + \chi_0 FSS + \chi_1 KH \cdot FSS_{lt} + \lambda_2 TSL_{lt} + \lambda_3 Ind + \lambda_4 Yr$$

Variable	All Subsidiaries		Majority-Owned Subsidiaries	
	Equations			
	(6.2)	(6.4)	(6.2)	(6.4)
Intercept	−0.0029	−0.0027	−0.009	−0.0004
	(−2.545)*	(−2.368)*	(−1.625)	(−3.072)**
FSS	−0.0037	−0.0036	−0.0019	−0.0016
	(−3.644)	(−3.408)	(−4.043)	(−3.290)
KH· FSS	—	0.0241	—	0.0278
		(3.045)**		(3.072)**
TSL	0.0036	0.0033	0.0047	0.0013
	(3.492)**	(3.079)**	(3.636)**	(2.480)*
Ind	−0.0006	−0.0003	−0.0006	−0.0003
	(−2.619)**	(−1.248)	(−2.670)**	(−1.070)
Yr	0.0002	0.0003	0.0002	0.0002
	(1.517)	(1.862)*	(1.417)	(1.283)
Adjusted R^2	0.184	0.328	0.217	0.277
N	112	98	111	95

Note: LCS = the parent's licensing receipts from unrelated foreign firms;
FSS = foreign subsidiary sales;
KH = R&D expenditures as a percentage of the parent's total sales;
TSL = the parent's total sales;
Ind = the industry dummy variable.
The t-statistics for testing the null hypothesis $\chi = \lambda = 0$ are presented in parentheses below the coefficients. *Significant at 5% level. **Significant at 1% level.

λ_2 coefficient on the control variable *TSL* is positive and significant. The χ_0 coefficient on *FSS* remains negative and significant, although the level of significance is reduced. However, the χ_1 coefficient on *FSS·KH* is found to be significantly greater than zero. A positive χ_1 on the interaction term means that the relationship between FDI and licensing varies across firms of different R&D intensity and is more positive for the firms with higher levels of R&D spending. Given negative χ_0 and χ_1, the relationship between FDI and licensing is negative for the firms with lower levels of R&D spending, but it becomes greater in numerical value for firms with higher levels of R&D spending. Recall that the full model is constructed by substituting coefficient λ_1 on *FSS* by $\lambda_1 = \chi_0 + \chi_1 KH$. Notice that the estimation for χ_0 and χ_1 respectively are -0.0016 and 0.0278 for majority-owned subsidiaries. Therefore, coefficient λ_1, or the overall association between FDI and licensing, becomes positive for the firms with R&D spending representing more than 5.8% of total sales. Overall, the results conclude hypothesis H1b. We may further notice that, with the inclusion of an interaction term, the λ_3 coefficient on *Ind* is no longer significant. This means that firms in the manufacturing industries more actively pursue a licensing strategy probably because these firms invest more in the engineering aspect of know-how and create more know-how possessions for international transfer.

The findings suggest that MNEs with more foreign investment tend to have lower levels of licensing revenues, but the relationship between FDI and licensing appears to be more positive for MNEs in the know-how intensive industries. The results can be explained with the recognition of both internalization and FDI signaling theories. It suggests that FDI may have substitution as well as complementary effects on licensing. With the finding of a negative overall relationship, FDI may be a substitute for licensing in foreign expansion, which supports the internalization proposition. However, because the interaction between FDI and know-how intensity is positive, it further suggests that the complementary effect of FDI signaling also exists, with a firm's FDI having a promotional effect on its licensing transactions. The net relation between FDI and licensing then is determined by the firm's level of know-how intensity, and it could be positive for firms with know-how intensity above a certain level. Therefore, the evidence is consistent with the FDI signaling proposition, suggesting that a firm's FDI internalization, with its perceptual influence on less-informed buyers, positively promotes its market transactions.

One major drawback of this study is that industrial aggregate data are used to examine the empirical relationships between foreign investment and licensing, and the results are then used to make interpretation at the firm level. We should be careful about such generalization. As a way to assess the soundness of this generalization, we further apply the firm-level data to examine the interrelations between the MNE's foreign investment and direct exports. The evidence on the relationships between FDI and licensing will be more solid if it is confirmed by the findings based on the firm-level study.

RELATIONSHIPS BETWEEN FDI AND EXPORTS

Based on the FDI signaling proposition, an MNE's foreign investment is further suggested to promote its transactions of finished products in the international markets.   One major implication in the context of equation (6.1) is that an increase of *FSS*, the MNE's foreign subsidiary sales, will lead to an increase in *XPT*, its exports to unaffiliated foreign firms.   The interrelations between these two variables are then postulated by hypotheses H2a and H2b, which direct development of empirical models to examine statistical relationships between MNEs' foreign investment and direct exports.

Specification of the Empirical Model

The basic empirical model with which to determine the relationship between FDI and direct export is

$$XPT_{it} = \beta_{0i} + \beta_1 FSS_{it} + \beta_2 DSL_{it} + \beta_3 IG_{it} + \beta_4 FX_t + \varepsilon_{it}, \qquad (6.5)$$

where XPT_{it} is the direct exports by MNE i, FSS_{it} is its foreign subsidiary sales, DSL_{it} is its domestic sales, IG_{it} is the worldwide growth of MNE i's industry, and FX_t is the rate of change for yearly average exchange rates in year t. While the time-series cross-sectional data are pooled to increase the number of observations, all the firm-level variables are expressed by growth rates to reduce the undesirable statistical properties of heteroskedasticity, autocorrelation, and nonstationarity.   Furthermore, the generalized least squares (GLS) method is applied to improve estimation of regression coefficients.

Hypothesis H2a proposes a positive association between the firm's *XPT* and *FSS*, thus predicting the β_{1i} coefficient to be significantly greater than zero. The model further includes variables *DSL*, *IG*, and *FX* to control the variation of dependent variables explained by the firm's expansion scale, industry growth, and exchange rate variability, respectively. Furthermore, Hypothesis H2b suggests that the association between *XPT* and *FSS* should be more positive for firms with a higher level of know-how intensity. Empirically, it predicts that the β_{1i} coefficient varies cross-sectionally and is more positively significant for firms with a higher level of R&D spending. This relation can be expressed as

$$\beta_{1i} = \gamma_0 + \gamma_1 KH_i + \eta_i, \qquad (6.6)$$

where KH_i is the know-how intensity of firm i, and the γ_1 coefficient is expected to be positive. Alternatively, this relationship can be investigated by substituting equation (6.6) into (6.5); that is,

$$XPT_{it} = \beta_0 + \gamma_0 FSS_{it} + \gamma_1 KH_i \cdot FSS_{it} + \beta_2 DSL_{it} + \beta_3 IG_{it} + \beta_4 FX_t + \varepsilon_{it}. \qquad (6.7)$$

For the same reason as that to justify equation (6.4), only the full model of equation (6.7) will be applied, and hypotheses H2a and H2b predict both γ_0 and γ_1 to be significantly greater than zero.

Sample and Measurement of Variables

The main sources of the firm-level data are *The World Directory of Multinational Enterprises* (Stopford 1982, Stopford et al. 1980). The books contain accounting data on 500 major multinational enterprises worldwide from 1975 to 1981 and include the export data for some firms. However, only those U.S. MNEs that have reported export data are selected for this study. This is because direct export is defined as the parent firm's sales to unaffiliated foreigners in this study. The U.S. multinational firms follow the accounting procedures established by the Financial Accounting Standard Board (FASB) in preparing their annual reports. The FASB issued the SFAS No. 14, *Financial Reporting for Segments of a Business Enterprise* (FASB 1976), requiring the exports reported to be the U.S. parent's exports to unaffiliated foreigners. The accounting data produced according to this rule thus satisfy the criterion of this study. MNEs from other countries follow different accounting standards and may aggregate the interfirm and intrafirm exports. To ensure that the relationship under investigation truly is between FDI and interfirm trade, only U.S. MNEs are included in the sample. As a result, a sample is formed with a total of 115 U.S. multinationals, which all have provided direct export data in their annual reports in the 1975–81 period.

The dependent variable XPT_{it}, measured by the firm's direct exports to unaffiliated foreigners, is the proxy for external market transactions of finished products. SFAS No. 14 mandates U.S. firms to provide separate disclosure for exports when they represent 10% or more of total sales. Consequently, although some firms have reported direct exports representing less than 10% of total sales, most firms in the sample have substantial exports. As such, there may be a selection bias in sample formation, which could result in an undesirable effect on the external validity of the study. The consequence may be that the findings only reflect the attributes of MNEs with substantial involvement in direct exports and may or may not be generalized to describe all MNEs.

The variable FSS_{it}, measured by total foreign subsidiary sales, is a proxy for the foreign production scale. Alternatively, a firm's FDI position was measured by its foreign assets and net income in previous studies. These two variables, however, are proxies associated with more measurement error. A measure based on the firm's foreign assets is less acceptable because the book value of assets is reported on a historical cost basis in the annual report. Thus, this measure may lead to systematic understatement of the FDI position for firms with a longer history. A measure of foreign production based on a foreign income variable also has more noise because it is directly affected by accounting rules and income tax laws, which vary across different host countries. These two variables are more subject to measurement error. Consequently, we choose the foreign subsidiary sales as the measure of foreign production scale. The variable DSL_{it} is a variable that controls for the total expansion of the firm and is measured by the MNE's total domestic sales in the corresponding period. The annual data for the 1975–81 period are used for this study.

The variable KH_i is a proxy for know-how intensity and is measured by the firm's spending on R&D as a percentage of total sales, the data are retrieved from the Industrial Compustat Annual tapes. The variable IG is used to control the export variation attributed to industry growth and is measured by the rate of change in the industry's worldwide output index. The data are obtained from the *Industrial Statistics Yearbook* published by the United Nations. The variable FX is used to control for the fluctuation of exports attributed to the strength of the MNE's home currency. The measurement is the nominal effective exchange rate of U.S. dollars, which is the trade-weighted exchange rate with the weights derived from the Multilateral Exchange Rate Model (MERM). A more detailed explanation of MERM rates can be found in Appendix C. The yearly average MERM rates are collected from various issues of *International Financial Statistics* published by the International Monetary Fund.

Results and Interpretation

Table 6.2 presents the attributes and industry composition of 115 U.S. multinationals in the sample. These firms vary in size, with a mean sales of $3.5 billion, and are mainly from the chemicals, machinery, electrical appliances, and electronics industries. This sample is representative of the

Table 6.2
Industry Composition and Characteristics of MNEs with Direct Exports

	Industry	SIC Code	Number
1.	Mining	10–14	2
2.	Food and beverage	20	6
3.	Tobacco	21	2
4.	Textile	22	1
5.	Wood and paper products	24–26	8
6.	Chemicals (except 283, 284)	28	19
7.	Drug and health products	283, 284	8
8.	Petroleum and related industries	29	4
9.	Rubber and plastic products	30	2
10.	Stone, clay, and glass	32	3
11.	Metals and metal products	33–34	7
12.	Machinery (except 357)	35	13
13.	Office computing machinery	357	9
14.	Electric equipment and electronics	36	15
15.	Transportation equipment (except 372,376)	37	6
16.	Aircraft and space vehicles	372, 276	3
17.	Other industries	38, 39, 49, 78	5
	Total		115

Variables	Mean	Median	Standard Deviation	Minimum Value	Maximum Value
Total sales	3,553	2,285	3,787	492	29,070
Domestic sales	2,286	1,488	2,348	175	1,7827
Foreign subsidiary sales	967	544	1,403	18	13,954
Direct exports	353	210	491	10	3,828
R&D/total sales (%)	2.98	2.43	2.28	0.07	14.92

Note: SIC Code = Standard Industry Classification Code.
All in $ million except R&D/total sales.

general population of multinationals, which are large and concentrated mainly in research-and skill-intensive industries.

Table 6.3
Correlation Matrix for Exports and Associated Variables

	XPT	FSS	KH· FSS	DSL	FX	IG
XPT	1.000					
FSS	0.349**	1.000				
KH· FSS	0.365**	0.777**	1.000			
DSL	0.113*	0.286**	0.234**	1.000		
FX	-0.132**	-0.350**	-0.282**	0.051	1.000	
IG	0.029	0.068	0.217**	-0.037	-0.352**	1.000

Note: *XPT* = the parent's direct exports;
       FSS = foreign subsidiary sales;
       DSL = the parent's domestic sales;
       KH = know-how intensity measured by R&D spending;
       FX = the rate of change in the yearly average MERM rate;
       IG = the industry worldwide growth.
     *Significant at 5% level. **Significant at 1% level.

The correlation matrix is displayed in Table 6.3. The bivariate analysis reflects the relationships between various variables, and it finds that *XPT* is positively correlated with *FSL*, *KH·FSS*, and *DSL*. Variable *XPT* is also found to be negatively correlated with *FX*. While an increase (decrease) in the value of the MERM index represents an appreciation (depreciation) of the U.S. dollar, the relationship shows that the U.S. export business is adversely affected by the strength of the dollar, as suggested by the theory. The variable *FSS* is also found to have a strong correlation with *DSL* and *FX*. This is somewhat expected, since a firm's foreign operations should be linked to the performance of the whole firm and be affected by general economic conditions. The strong correlation between the independent variables further indicates the need for multiple regression analyses, which estimate the relationship between exports and foreign production by controlling the effects of other related variables.

The results of multiple regression analysis, including estimated coefficients and *t*-statistics, are further summarized in Table 6.4. The third column reports the results from applying the regression model from equation (6.5). As indicated, the regression coefficients of control variables *DSL,*

Table 6.4

Cross-Sectional Regression Analysis of MNEs' Export and Foreign Investment by $XPT_{it} = \beta_0 + \gamma_0 FSS + \gamma_1 KH \cdot FSS + \beta_2 DSL + \beta_3 IG + \beta_4 FX$

Variable	Explanation	Equation (6.5)	Equation (6.7)
Intercept		6.930 (2.685)**	8.552 (3.252)**
FSS	The parent's direct exports	0.403 (6.759)**	0.191 (2.113)*
KH· FSS	The interaction between FSS and R&D spending	——	0.092 (3.173)**
DSL	The parent's domestic sales	0.006 (0.086)	0.000 (0.001)
FX	The rate of change of yearly MERM rates	0.078 (0.451)	0.035 (0.199)
IG	The industry worldwide growth rate	0.274 (0.736)	−0.077 (−0.199)
Adjusted R^2		0.114	0.134
N		417	413

Note: The t-statistics for testing null hypothesis $\gamma = \beta = 0$ are presented in parentheses below the coefficients. *Significant at 5% level. **Significant at 1% level.

FX, and GI are all insignificant in the model. Furthermore, the regression coefficient on FSS is positive with significant t-statistics ($P < 0.000$). This suggests that foreign production complements direct exports for the whole sample. The findings support hypothesis H2a that the MNE's expansion of foreign production has a positive association with its direct export sales.

The fourth column in Table 6.4 further reports the regression results based on the empirical model presented in equation (6.7). The γ_1 coefficient on the interaction of foreign production and R&D spending is significantly greater than zero ($P < 0.001$), indicating a more positive association between FDI and direct exports for firms with higher levels of R&D spending. Furthermore, with the inclusion of the interaction term, the γ_0 coefficient remains significant, but its significance level is reduced ($P < 0.035$). This indicates that the overall relation between FDI and direct exports is complementary, but the positive coefficient on *FSS* in equation (6.5) is mainly attributed to a strong connection between FDI and exports of R&D-intensive firms. The findings are consistent with hypothesis H2b, suggesting that foreign investment by know-how-intensive firms is more positively associated with their direct exports. Therefore, the test results conclude both hypotheses H2a and H2b. The interpretation in the FDI signaling framework is that the firm's FDI boosts its external market transactions of finished products, because it alters the buyers' perceptions and stimulates the market demand.

SUMMARY

In this chapter, we investigated empirically the proposed FDI signaling effects, mainly by examining the relationships between the MNE's foreign investment and licensing sales, and between its FDI and direct exports. First, we found a negative relationship between the U.S. firm's foreign production and licensing to unaffiliated foreigners, which supports the internalization argument that FDI overall may have a substitution effect on licensing. We further found that the interaction term between foreign production and know-how variables is positive and significant, which confirms the FDI signaling proposition that FDI in effect may promote the market transactions of know-how. A plausible explanation for these findings is that there is a coexistence of substitution effect of internalization and complementary effect of FDI signaling, and the observed empirical relationships represent a net result of these two effects. The implications of the evidence are that the FDI expansion of know-how intensive firms may well come with a growth of market transactions of know-how. Second, we found a positive association between FDI and direct exports, which indicates that the MNE's foreign investment promotes its exports to unaffiliated foreigners. Furthermore, we also found a positive interaction term between FDI and know-how intensity, indicating that foreign production by know-how intensive firms may have a greater promotional effect on their market transactions of final products. In summary, the study results based on the MNE's operations in the licensing and export markets are consistent with the FDI signaling proposition, which suggests that the firm's expansion of foreign production is a signal positively influencing the market perception of the firm-specific know-how and thus promoting its market transactions of intermediate know-how products and finished products embodying know-how.

There are methodological limitations in the empirical studies of this chapter. First, industry aggregate data were applied to investigate the relations between FDI and licensing, and the results were then used to make interpretations at the firm level. This approach critically depends on the assumption that industry-level data are representative of firms in the industry. We should be careful about such a generalization. However, our findings become more convincing when consistent results are found on the relationships between FDI and direct exports in our study based on firm-level data. The second drawback is that this study applies regression analysis to examine the effects of MNEs' internalization on its externalization. The empirical findings support the proposition that the FDI action has more positive effects on direct exports and licensing sales of firms with more intensive know-how. However, it should be made clear that such a cause-and-effect relationship is not established on regression results but derived from the FDI signaling theory. While the regression method can be used to determine the existence of concomitant variations between two variables, it is incapable of identifying which of these two is a causal factor. Finally, in determining the effects of FDI on direct exports and licensing, we considered the internalization substitution and the FDI signaling complement as two major relationships between FDI and market transactions. Consequently, we interpreted the evidence as supportive of the FDI signaling proposition. However, there might be some alternative explanations for these relationships. This requires a future study to include more control variables to exclude some other specific causes. Therefore, additional studies are required to have more conclusive results, particularly because relationships between the MNE's various involvements is measured in a relatively lengthy time horizon and thus can be affected by various internal and external variables. It would be a difficult task to remove all other possible effects to determine the signaling element. As such, the event study method is more powerful because it measures the instant market response, and the cause-effect relationship between a signal and its market effects can be explicitly established. In Chapter 7 we will further examine the FDI signaling effect and its consequence in the stock market valuation.

NOTES

1. The substitute effect of FDI is more relevant to the case in which a firm serves a country market with one major product and by both direct exports and local production. This is the basis for the argument (e.g., Contractor and Safafi-nejad 1981) that a firm's increasing use of market arrangements for know-how transfer will lead to disinternalization of its external markets in the long term.

2. Casson (1987) suggests that a firm's establishment of foreign production signals its commitment to that foreign market, implying that this investment will promote its market transactions there. However, he does not distinguish between the foreign subsidiary sales, which are a measure of internalization, and the parent firm's direct exports, which are a measure of market transactions. Aharoni (1966) proposes that a firm's foreign production may increase the brand recognition in foreign countries, thus promoting the market for its direct exports. In this case, there is an implicit recognition of the perceptual impact of the FDI action in the foreign market.

7

FDI Announcement
and Its Valuation Effects

In an efficient capital market, stock prices will adjust rapidly to newly arrived information, and the information content of a firm's action thus can be determined by the stock price changes in response to that action. Therefore, in finance a general approach to test the signaling effect is to examine the stock market reaction to a firm's signal action. The purpose of this chapter is to investigate empirically the FDI signaling proposition by detecting the stock price correction associated with MNEs' public announcements of foreign investment. We first apply the event study method to examine FDI valuation effects, and then undertake multiple regression analyses to identify the sources of these effects. The FDI valuation modeling in Chapter 5 generates implications that provide us guidance to develop testable hypotheses and an empirical design.

HYPOTHESES AND PRIOR LITERATURE

The FDI signaling valuation model in Chapter 5 has established a conceptual link between FDI and the firm's valuation, which suggests that the value of the firm, while reflecting all the public information on the firm's earnings prospects, should incorporate the additional information conveyed by the firm's FDI action. Empirically this suggests that the firm's FDI move should affect its stock prices in a systematic manner, which allows us to investigate the proposed FDI signaling effect based on the stock market movement. The recognition of the complicated effects of FDI further leads us to formulate hypotheses with which to differentiate the signaling effect from other possible sources of valuation effects.

Hypothesized Information Content of Foreign Direct Investment

The efficient market hypothesis suggests that the stock price fully reflect all publicly available information. The driving force underlying this concept is the motivation for profits—individual investors and other market participants are motivated to seek information from various sources, and competition sets stock prices such that on average investors can only earn the same risk-adjusted rate of return from trading on publicly available information. The efficient market hypothesis is generally accepted and assumed to be valid, and it plays a critically important role in empirical finance. Its importance lies in providing a basis to test many economic theories. Based on this concept, we can investigate the cause-and-effect relationship associated with foreign investment. If the FDI signaling proposition is correct that the firm's FDI action has information content, then the firm's disclosure of its FDI decision should have an immediate effect on the market value of the firm. Since public corporations often make public announcements prior to their moves to enter certain foreign markets, we can test the theory by examining stock price adjustments in response to FDI announcements. Based on Proposition 6a, it can be hypothesized that

Hypothesis H3a: There is an increase of firm value at the firm's FDI announcements, ceteris paribus.

The confirmation of this hypothesis may not be exclusively interpreted in the context of the FDI signaling proposition, as is suggested by the discussion presented at the beginning of Chapter 6. This is because the valuation effect can be attributed to other effects of foreign investment. In this study, we seek to identify the stock price variation representing the information about firm-specific know-how, but this variation may also result from operational benefits and costs of FDI. For example, a firm's foreign expansion may bring some international diversification gains, or develop a multinational network that provides the firm with a collection of valuable options (Kogut 1983), or change the firm's opportunity setting in terms of returns and risk. While the investment may have an overall effect on the performance of the firm, the question is whether these effects can be sources of the valuation effect. With the possible existence of these operational consequences, hypothesis H3a can no longer effectively differentiate the FDI signaling proposition. Therefore, additional hypotheses need to be developed. Based on Proposition 7 in Chapter 5, we hypothesize that

Hypothesis H3b: The value increase at FDI announcements is greater in magnitude for firms with higher levels of R&D spending, ceteris paribus.

Hypothesis H3b can be explained intuitively. As the internalization theory suggests, a major aspect of market imperfections should be the imperfect information associated with know-how transactions. Obviously, it is more difficult to value a firm correctly if its know-how intangible assets constitute a larger portion of total assets value. Therefore, if the FDI announcement truly conveys information about the intangible assets, it should lead to more substantial price adjustments for firms with more intensive know-how. While hypothesis H3b is consistent with the hypothesized information element of FDI announcements, the association between the FDI valuation effect and know-how intensity can be attributed to FDI signaling only with the expected FDI earnings being controlled. This is to control for the earnings effects predicted by both internalization and industrial organization theorists: The former believes that this valuation effect reflects the higher profit from internalization of intangible assets, and the latter attributes it to the firm's market power, i.e., know-how-intensive firms can extract more monopoly rents from FDI expansion.

This is an essential part of the FDI signaling test, which seeks to differentiate the stock price change that reflects the revaluation of existing intangible assets from that attributed to the expected foreign earnings increase. Empirically, we should not only show that the stock price reaction to FDI news is greater for know-how intensive firms, but also that it cannot be explained by the expected earnings effect. This is the implication stated by Proposition 6b and is formulated in the hypothesis as follows:

Hypothesis H3c: *The positive association between the FDI valuation effect and know-how intensity exists even after the exclusion of the valuation effect associated with expected foreign earnings.*

This hypothesis suggests that the FDI valuation effect based on know-how intensity remains after we remove the price adjustment reflecting the expected future earnings. Consequently, we can conclude that this value adjustment represents the new information associated with the valuation of intangible assets. This would confirm the FDI signaling proposition, suggesting that the FDI announcement would convey information about the firm's know-how based intangible assets. Hypotheses H3a, H3b, and H3c jointly provide a framework for testing the FDI signaling theory.

Prior Empirical Research

There is an extensive literature on the empirical relationship between a firm's FDI operations and performance in the stock market. Agmon and

Lessard (1977) found that the correlation between the stock returns of U.S. multinationals and the world market index is positively associated with the degree of foreign involvement measured by foreign sales. Jacquillat and Solnik (1978) compared the variability of investment returns of two portfolios: One is an international portfolio diversified into major national stock markets, and the other is formed with U.S. multinationals, with a portfolio of purely domestic U.S. firms as a benchmark. The findings suggest that, whereas significant risk reduction has been accomplished by diversifying internationally, only insubstantial diversificational gains can be obtained by investing in a portfolio of U.S. multinationals. The study undertaken by Senchack and Beedles (1980) led to a similar conclusion. The early empirical research focuses primarily on the diversification aspect of FDI, and the evidence shows the existence of FDI diversification to a certain extent.

Fatemi (1984) applied an event study based on monthly return data and failed to find any abnormal performance in the stock market around the period of the firms' foreign expansion. The study by Doukas and Travlos (1988) generated the same result but finds that a U.S. firm's stock prices experience positive gains when it expands to a country in which the firm has no previous presence. While the operational advantage of the MNE has been well recognized, why do these studies fail to identify the stock market reaction to FDI announcements? The explanation by Errunza and Senbet (1981, 1984) was that, in an efficient capital market, the advantages enjoyed by the MNE have been fully incorporated into the firm's stock prices and thus the MNE and domestic firm both provide the same risk-adjusted rate of return. Therefore, Errunza and Senbet turned to a market-value-based study and find a statistically significant association between the excess value of the firm and its degree of foreign involvements. Similar studies were also performed by Hirschey (1982a) and Kim and Lyn (1986). While the results confirmed earlier findings, they were interpreted predominantly in the industrial organization framework, which considers that the premium of the MNE's stock price is a reflection of its market power derived from its foreign investment.

The event study method was further employed by recent studies to examine the foreign investment resulting from mergers and acquisitions. Harris and Ravenscraft (1991) examined domestic and foreign acquisitions that took place in the United States from 1970 to 1987. The findings suggest that international takeovers are more likely to occur in R&D intensive industries, and by the foreign firms in related industries. International takeovers result in more value increases for the target firms in comparison with the domestic acquisitions and are more prosperous in the periods when the U.S. dollar is relatively weak. The study by Kang (1993) specifically examined Japanese MNEs' acquisitions of U.S. firms. The international investment is found to increase significantly the value of both Japanese bidders and U.S. targets, while the value increase of Japanese parent firms can be explained by the extent of leverage and bank control and the strength of the Japanese yen. Although these authors focus mainly on the imperfections in the financial markets, the findings are consistent with the predictions of both market power and internalization approaches.

Morch and Yeung sought to apply the market valuation approach to assess the internalization theory. Their findings suggest that a positive relationship exists between the value of the firm's intangible assets (based on Tobin's q ratio) and its level of foreign involvements, and that this relationship is more significant for the firm with a higher level of R&D and advertising spending (Morch and Yeung 1991). Furthermore, by applying an event study method, they found a positive relation between the abnormal return at the FDI announcement and the level of R&D and advertising spending (Morch and Yeung 1992). They argued that the findings support the internalization framework, indicating that a firm can enhance the value of intangible assets by internalization in foreign markets. However, the evidence produced in their studies does not provide exclusive support to the internalization theory. The findings in Morch and Yeung (1991) can be interpreted in both the internalization and industrial organization frameworks. As to the event study (Morch and Yeung 1992), the implication of the results is more complicated. The observed stock price gain at FDI and its pattern can be attributed either to the expected future foreign earnings (as suggested by Morch and Yeung), which would be consistent with both internalization and market power hypotheses, or the revaluation of intangible assets upon the information conveyed by the FDI announcement act, which supports the FDI signaling theory. Unfortunately, Morch and Yeung did not differentiate these different effects. The main point is that if their argument is correct that the FDI valuation effect reflects the foreign earnings prospect, the next issue still will be whether it is due to the internalization gain or the enhancement of the MNE's market power. No clue was provided in their studies. On the other hand, if we want to argue that this valuation effect is associated with FDI signaling, then the empirical model should be developed with additional control to eliminate the valuation effects reflecting foreign earnings and other possible operations effects.

EMPIRICAL DESIGN AND DATA

A standard event study procedure is performed to test the FDI signaling proposition in the context of market valuation of the firm. The event study method, by examining the firm's stock price behavior around the date of the event (that is, the firm adopts an observable move such as public disclosure), determines whether there is a systematic market reaction to the event. Any significant change in stock prices in the event period is then attributed to the information of the event. This information is either contained in the disclosure or conveyed by the action of disclosure (that is, the firm's willingness to adopt such an action tells the market something). Therefore, the event study method can be used to investigate the valuation effect of FDI announcements. Furthermore, we apply regression analysis to determine whether there are factors to explain the cross-sectional variation in the FDI valuation effect. In this section, we provide a brief description of the sample, variables, and sources of data.

Sample

We define an event as a firm's public disclosure of its foreign investment plan, which is identified from annual issues of the *Wall Street Journal Index* in the 1970–88 period. The event date refers to the earliest date the news was found in the newspaper article. Some FDI events seem to receive much publicity, judging by the number of times the news was covered. Therefore, these FDI moves might have been disclosed to the public by other media even before the news appeared in the *Wall Street Journal*. To ensure the accuracy of the date for these events, we further go back to concurrent issues of *Predicasts F & S Index United States*, which indexes business events by firms from a wide range of newspapers and journals. Of all the event firms, only those whose data are available in the Center for Research in Securities Price (CRSP) daily returns file are included in the sample. As a result, the final sample is formed with 161 announced FDI plans. In the whole sample, 49% of the entries are to new markets, and the rest represent expansion into the countries in which the firms have already had operations. Furthermore, 74% of these entries are in the form of acquisitions, and the others are through greenfield expansions. Around 43% of target regions are developed countries, 41% newly developed countries and oil export countries, and the rest are other developing countries. Table 7.1 reports the industry composition of the event firms and the time period of their foreign entries. A visual inspection shows that the FDI announcements are made by firms mainly from a few manufacturing industries, such as petroleum, metal, chemical, electrical equipment and electronics, and motor vehicles. This is consistent with the industry concentration of MNEs documented by prior studies. Furthermore, while MNEs in the primary industries were active in foreign involvements in the 1970s, MNEs in the electronics, financial services, and food and beverage industries seemed to play a leading role in foreign expansion in the 1980s.

Table 7.1
Industry Composition and FDI Event Periods

Industry	SIC Code	1970s	1980s	Total
1. Mining	10–14	5	1	6
2. Food, drink and tobacco	20, 21	2	7	9
3. Textile	22	0	1	1
4. Wood and paper products	24–26	2	3	5
5. Chemicals (except 283, 284)	28	14	5	19
6. Drug and health products	283, 284	5	2	7
7. Petroleum and related industries	29	7	9	16
8. Rubber and plastic products	30	0	2	2
9. Stone, clay, and glass	32	1	0	1
10. Metals and metal products	33–34	13	4	17
11. Machinery	35	2	2	4
12. Electric equip. and electronics	36	9	13	22
13. Transport. equip. (except 72, 376)	37	19	3	22
14. Aircraft and space vehicles	372, 376	0	2	2
15. Other manufacturing	38, 39	2	1	3
16. Finance	60–67	2	9	11
17. Other services	48–58, 70, 89	8	6	14
Total		95	66	161

Note: SIC Code = Standard Industry Classification Code.

Proxy Variables

A firm's know-how intensity is measured by its average level of R&D spending. Based on Statements of Financial Accounting Standards No. 2 *Accounting for Research and Development Costs* (FASB 1974), this expenditures is recognized as expense in the spending year. However, there is strong evidence showing a relationship between this expenditure and the firm value (Ben-Zion 1984, Chang et al. 1990, Cockburn and Griliches 1987, Griliches 1981, Hirschey 1982b, Pakes 1985). Furthermore, the firm's advertising expenditure is also found to be associated with the firm value. Therefore, these two variables have been widely used as proxies for intangible assets in prior studies. Such an approach essentially is to use an input measure as an estimation for an output proxy and is more subject to measurement error. Apparently, a firm with a higher level of spending on R&D and advertising does not necessarily create more advanced know-how.

Thus, these variables are imperfect proxies for know-how intangibles. In this chapter, the know-how intensity *KH* is measured by three-year average of R&D and advertising expenses as percentages of total sales. The source of the data is the Industry Compustat Annual tape. For those firms with missing values in these expense items, their spending is assumed to be zero.

The foreign earnings variable is used as a proxy for the firm's performance in foreign production. We are fully aware of the potential drawback in using accounting variables as proxies for the firm's real performance, particularly the performance in the foreign segment.[1] However, there are no other better proxies available for the purpose of this study. Furthermore, there is evidence showing a significant relationship between stock price changes and reported accounting earnings (Ball and Brown 1968, Beaver 1968, Beaver et al. 1979, 1980, Foster 1975, Grant 1980). A more recent study (Strong and Walker 1993), based on improved methodology, finds that the earnings variation can explain as much as 38% of stock price changes. Besides, our findings based on a large sample suggest that MNEs' foreign earnings performance measured by the rates of return on foreign assets and foreign sales is significantly associated with its know-how proxies.[2] While this result is consistent with existing economic theories, it further suggests that accounting earnings data of foreign segment have information. To estimate the market expectation of firms' foreign expansion, we adopt a naive expectation model, assuming that the market expects a firm's new foreign venture to earn profits equivalent to its existing foreign operations. We estimate *EFE*, the expected foreign earnings performance of the firm's new FDI alternatively by the three-year average of rates of return on foreign sales and on foreign assets three years after the FDI events, which are calculated by dividing the firm's foreign operating income by foreign sales and foreign assets. The foreign operating income is the earnings before taxes, which is not affected by the noise resulting from the variation of national taxation regulations across countries. The foreign operations data are obtained from the VALU Line database and *The World Scope: Industrial Company Profile*.

The dummy variable *DIV* is used to identify the FDI diversification effect by distinguishing the firm's entry to a new market from its expansion of existing foreign operations. Its value is determined by whether the firm has any existing subsidiary in the targeted foreign country in the year of the FDI announcement. The sources of information are various issues of *International Directory of Corporate Affiliation* (National Register Publishing Co. 1980) and *Directory of American Firms Operating in Foreign Countries* (Angel 1979), which provide names of all U.S. firms involved in foreign operations and lists of each firm's subsidiaries in foreign countries.

RESULTS AND INTERPRETATION

The Average Stock Price Reaction to FDI Announcements

The hypothesized information content of FDI will be confirmed if the evidence shows that the FDI announcement systematically affects the value of the firm, as suggested by Hypothesis 3a. The conclusion of this hypothesis should be based on a rejection of null hypothesis that firms' FDI announcements have no effect on their stock prices. First, the event-study method is applied to determine whether the firms experience abnormal returns in the event period.

Following Fama (1976), the market model can be specified as

$$R_{it} = a_i + b_i R_{mt} + e_{it}, \tag{7.1}$$

where $R_{it} = \ln(1 + r_{it})$ and r_{it} is the rate of return on the stock of firm i on event day t, $R_{mt} = \ln(1 + r_{mt})$ and r_{mt} is the market rate of return on event day t, and e_{it} is the error term of firm i on day t. Firms' daily stock returns and market rates of return, which are estimated by the equally weighted CRSP index, are obtained from the Center for Research in Securities Price (CRSP) tapes. The abnormal return is calculated by

$$AR_{it} = R_{it} - \hat{R}_{it} = R_{it} - (\hat{a}_i + \hat{b}_i R_{mt}), \tag{7.2}$$

$$t = -10, \ldots, +10.$$

where $\hat{R}_{it}$ is the expected rate of return for the stock of firm i on event day t, and $\hat{a}$, and $\hat{b}$ are the market model parameters estimated by ordinary least squares, with a 140-day period from $t = -150$ to $t = -11$.

This study follows the procedures reported in Patell (1976). The standardized daily abnormal returns (SAR) are calculated for each sample firm for the window period, with the abnormal daily returns divided by the residual standard error from the market model regression and a factor reflecting an increase in variance due to the prediction outside the estimating period. For a sample of N firms, the average standardized daily abnormal return ($ASAR$) for each event day is calculated by

$$ASAR_t = \frac{1}{N} \sum_{i=1}^{N} SAR_{it}. \tag{7.3}$$

The expected value of $ASAR_t$ is zero in the absence of abnormal performance. If the individual abnormal returns are normal and independent, $\sqrt{N} \cdot ASAR_t$ has a unit normal distribution. The test thus is based on the Z-

statistic to determine whether the average standardized abnormal return is statistically different from zero.

Table 7.2
Average Standardized Daily Abnormal Returns and Cumulative Abnormal Returns in the Event Period

Event Day	AR	Z-value	CAR	Z-Value
-10	-0.026	-0.194	-0.026	-0.194
-9	0.034	0.820	0.009	0.443
-8	0.097	0.520	0.105	0.880
-7	0.035	0.334	0.140	0.929
-6	0.011	0.067	0.151	0.861
-5	0.123	1.136	0.274	1.250
-4	-0.007	0.089	0.267	1.191
-3	-0.203	-1.498	0.064	0.584
-2	0.058	0.042	0.122	0.564
-1	-0.069	-0.287	0.053	0.445
0	0.121	0.675	0.174	0.627
+1	-0.104	-0.340	0.070	0.503
+2	0.289	2.213**	0.358	1.097
+3	0.096	0.990	0.454	1.321
+4	-0.117	-0.861	0.338	1.054
+5	0.057	0.694	0.395	1.194
+6	0.200	1.498	0.595	1.522
+7	-0.153	-1.071	0.442	1.227
+8	-0.140	-1.169	0.301	0.926
+9	0.097	0.196	0.398	0.946
+10	0.288	1.560	0.686	1.264

Note: Average standardized daily abnormal returns (*ASAR*) and Z-values, and cumulative standardized abnormal Returns (*CAR*) and Z-values for 161 U.S. firms for ten days before and after the date of FDI announcement (day -10 to day +10). On a two-tailed test, *Significant at 5% level. **Significant at 1% level.

Table 7.2 summarizes the test results for the whole sample. The first column displays the window period of eleven days (-10 to +10). The second and third columns report the average standardized daily abnormal returns and their Z-statistics, and the fourth and fifth columns further present the eleven-day cumulative standardized abnormal returns and their Z-statistics, for the hypothesis test. The average daily abnormal returns are found statistically insignificant on the event day (0). The cumulative abnormal returns are also insignificant for the window period. Consequently, the test results fail to reject the null hypothesis and to conclude that FDI announcements affect stock prices.

Such results are not surprising, given the similar findings documented by prior studies (Doukas and Travlos 1988, Fatemi 1984, Morch and Yeung 1991). On the surface, the evidence indicates that FDI announcements do not affect the value of the firm, as the firm's disclosure of its FDI intention would not alter investors' expectations of the firm. However, there is also evidence showing varied stock price reactions among different firm groups. For example, Doukas and Travlos (1988) found that the firm's stock price has a gain when it expands to a new country market, and Morch and Yeung (1992) found that the abnormal returns at FDI announcements are positively related to the firm's R&D and advertising spending. Thus, a more plausible explanation is that the benefits and costs of foreign investment vary across firms of different natures. As such, the market reacts differently to the FDI announcements of different firms, and the FDI valuation effect varies across firms. The valuation effect, however, may be averaged out when it is estimated by a sample consisting of all firms, and the results thus is insignificant. Therefore, the evidence does not necessarily contradict the proposed FDI valuation effect but requires additional analysis on this effect.

FDI Valuation Effect Associated with Know-How Intensity

Hypothesis H3b holds that the stock price reaction to FDI announcements is greater for the firms with higher levels of know-how intensity, which will be accepted if the evidence rejects the null hypothesis that this reaction has no systematic difference among firms of different know-how intensity. The hypothesis test is performed on samples partitioned according to the know-how criterion, with the group of lower know-how intensity consisting of forty-four event firms whose spending on R&D and advertising represents less than 2% of total sales, and the know-how-intensive group consisting of sixty-two event firms whose spending on R&D and advertising represents more than 5% of total sales. The average standardized daily abnormal returns and cumulative standardized abnormal returns are estimated separately for two groups for an eleven-day period (-5 to +5).

Table 7.3 reports the test results for the partitioned MNE samples. Panel A summarizes the average daily abnormal returns, the cumulative abnormal returns, and the Z-statistics for the firms with a lower level of know-how intensity. The average daily abnormal return on the event day (0) has a negative sign but is statistically insignificant. The cumulative abnormal returns are also insignificant during the window period. Panel B

Table 7.3
Average and Cumulative Standardized Abnormal Returns for the Partitioned MNE Groups in the Event Period

Event Day	AR	Z-value	CAR	Z-value
(A) Firms of lower know-how intensity (N = 44)				
-5	-0.124	-1.172	-0.124	-1.172
-4	-0.107	-0.262	-0.230	0.064
-3	-0.407	-1.500	-0.638	-0.814
-2	0.086	0.456	-0.551	0.477
-1	-0.246	-0.867	-0.797	-0.814
0	-0.254	-1.058	-1.051	-1.175
+1	-0.546	-1.714	-1.597	-1.736
+2	0.482	1.057	-1.115	-1.250
+3	-0.259	-0.274	-1.374	-1.270
+4	0.091	0.481	-1.283	-1.053
+5	0.158	0.429	-1.125	-0.874
(B) Firms of higher know-how intensity (N = 62)				
-5	0.026	0.217	0.026	0.217
-4	0.217	0.990	0.243	0.853
-3	-0.104	-0.628	0.139	0.994
-2	0.400	1.459	0.539	1.019
-1	0.004	-0.090	0.543	0.871
0	0.532	2.229**	1.076	1.705
+1	0.262	1.600	1.338	2.184**
+2	0.087	0.678	1.425	2.282**
+3	0.311	1.432	1.736	2.629***
+4	-0.280	-0.899	1.456	2.210**
+5	0.035	0.319	1.491	2.203**

Note: Firms of lower know-how intensity have R&D and advertising spending less than 2% of total sales; firms of higher know-how intensity have R&D and advertising spending more than 5% of sales.

On a two-tailed test, *Significant at 10% level, **Significant at 5% level, and ***Significant at 1% level.

reports the abnormal returns for the firms with a higher level of know-how intensity. The average abnormal return on day 0 is found to be 0.532% and significant at the 5% level on a two-tailed test. The cumulative abnormal returns are also positively significant at the 5% level after the event day. Figure 7.1 further presents a graphic picture of eleven-day (-5 to +5) cumulative abnormal returns for two groups, which clearly shows different stock price behaviors for two firm groups in the window period. Based on the statistical results, therefore, we reject the null hypothesis to conclude the alternative hypothesis H3b that the FDI announcement has a more positive effect on firms with a higher level of know-how intensity.

Figure 7.1
The Valuation Effect of FDI Announcements for Partitioned MNE Groups

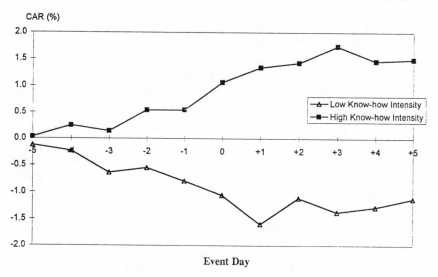

Event Day

Note: The low know-how intensity group consists of firms with R&D and advertising spending representing less than 2% of total sales, and the high know-how intensity group consists
of firms with R&D and advertising spending representing more than 5% of total sales.
    CAR = Cumulative standardized abnormal returns.

The results show that only FDI announcements made by know-how intensive firms lead to value increases. This finding is consistent with the FDI signaling proposition, suggesting that FDI action reveals information about firm-specific know-how. In an efficient market, the new information is incorporated into stock prices instantly in the market valuation of the firm's intangible assets.

However, the evidence is also subject to alternative interpretations. Morch and Yeung (1992) believed that foreign production by know-how-intensive firms is systematically more profitable; that is, the valuation effect reflects future FDI earnings. This view, however, is the conclusion derived from the evidence. Based on their research design, it is unclear whether the FDI valuation effect represents a marginal price correction reflecting the foreign earnings prospect or a revaluation of the firm's assets based on new information. The issue can be more clearly seen with a reference to the FDI valuation model in Chapter 5. As shown in equation (5.34), the value of the firm with foreign investment V_2 can be expressed as the sum of two terms on the right side of the equation. More specifically, any stock price change can be associated with either the value of foreign assets (the second term) or the value of the domestic assets (the first term), or both.

The existing research on the multinational enterprise focuses exclusively on the second term, seeking to identify various benefits associated with the FDI valuation effect. While Morch and Yeung (1992) found the FDI valuation effect in the event period, they attempt to interpret the evidence in the internalization framework. That explanation, however, contradicts the argument presented by Errunza and Senbet (1981); that is, the advantages enjoyed by the MNE should have been recognized by the market and fully incorporated into the stock prices in an efficient market. Furthermore, if the FDI valuation effect is interpreted as a reflection of FDI earnings prospects, the evidence again is subject to alternative explanations. The claim may also be made by the industrial organization approach because R&D and advertising variables are major proxies for the firm's market power. Our conjecture is that at least part of this valuation effect is attributed to the FDI signaling consequence, resulting from revaluation of the firm's intangible assets based on information contained in FDI announcements. This proposition can be further examined.

Determinants of Cumulative Abnormal Returns

The test of the FDI signaling effect, therefore, should be based on hypothesis H3c, which proposes that the FDI valuation effect may not be attributed to the foreign earnings prospect. The FDI signaling proposition will be concluded only if evidence rejects the null hypothesis that the observed FDI valuation effect associated with know-how-intensive firms is entirely explained by the FDI earnings prospect. This test is necessary because of the empirical relationship between the firm's know-how-intensity and foreign earnings performance (see note 2). Based on this evidence, it can be argued that the observed stock price pattern is a reflection of the earnings effect, that is, the market reacts more favorably to FDI announce-ments of know-how intensive firms because it expects their future FDI to be more profitable. Therefore, the essence of the FDI signaling test is to show that the relationship between the FDI valuation effect and know-how intensity remains significant after removing the price adjustment reflecting the expected FDI earnings. Only based on such evidence, can we conclude that revaluation reflects information about know-how intangible assets.

A cross-sectional regression analysis is applied to examine the relationship between the abnormal returns at FDI announcements and know-how intensity, with expected foreign earnings and other major variables being controlled. The empirical model is specified as

$$CAR_i = \beta_0 + \beta_1 EFE_i + \beta_2 DIV_i + \beta_3 ECN_i + \beta_4 MODE_i + \beta_5 KH_i + \varepsilon_i, \qquad (7.4)$$

where CAR is two-day (-1 to 0) cumulative standardized abnormal returns; EFE is the expected foreign earnings performance; DIV is the diversification dummy variable equal to 1 for an entry to a new market and 0 for expansion of an existing market; ECN is the economic region dummy variable equal to 2 for a developed country, 1 for a newly developed country or an oil exporting country, and 0 for a developing country; $MODE$ is the entry-mode dummy variable equal to 0 for greenfield and 1 for foreign acquisition; and KH is the measure of know-how intensity.

In the regression model, the β_1 coefficient should be greater than zero to explain the FDI valuation effect by the expected FDI earnings, and the β_2 coefficient should be greater than zero to support the diversification gain argument. Variables ECN and $MODE$ are to control the valuation effects associated with economic stages of target countries and entry modes, and the signs of β_3 and β_4 are not predetermined. Finally, KH is the variable that captures the FDI signaling effect, and the regression coefficient β_5 is explicitly predicted to be positive and significant by the signaling proposition.

Table 7.4 reports the regression results with different measures of EFE, the expected foreign earnings and know-how intensity. First, the β_1 coefficient on EFE is found insignificant, with the expected foreign earnings to be estimated either by returns on foreign assets or returns on foreign sales. This finding is rather surprising as it is contradictory to the common belief. The first question coming to our mind is whether the proxy variable is wrong. In other words, do foreign accounting earnings in any way measure the firm's foreign performance at all? It is true that, with the limitation of accounting data, the measure based on foreign operating earnings is likely to be a noisy proxy. However, since the evidence suggests a strong association between the firm's foreign earnings measure and know-how proxies and confirms existing MNE theories (see note 2), we conclude that foreign earnings data have information content. Therefore, the finding of insignificant relation between CAR and EFE concludes that the

Table 7.4
Cross-Sectional Regression Analysis of Two-Day CAR at FDI Announcements

Variable	(1)	(2)	(3)	(4)
Intercept	-2.745	-2.832	-2.455	-2.529
	(-2.058)	(-2.111)	(-1.657	(-1.904)
EFE	-0.001	-0.007	-0.019	-0.017
	(-0.409)	(-0.321)	(-0.910)	(-0.833)
DIV	1.117	1.171	1.123	1.172
	(1.955)**	(2.209)**	(1.971)**	(2.037)**
ECN	0.654	0.670	0.604	0.620
	(1.448)	(1.479)	(1.330)	(1.360)
MODE	-0.166	-0.165	-0.238	-0.234
	(-0.247)	(-0.245)	(-0.354)	(-0.354)
*KH*1	——	0.444	——	0.433
		(2.262)**		(2.250)**
*KH*2	——	0.232	——	0.235
		(1.200)		(1.220)
*KH*2	0.337	——	0.334	——
	(2.618)***		(2.665)***	
R^2	0.083	0.086	0.087	0.090

Note: *EFE* = the expected foreign earnings performance, estimated by foreign operating income/foreign sales in columns 1 and 2, foreign operating income/foreign assets in 3 and 4;

DIV = the diversification dummy variable;
ECN = the dummy for the economic stage of a target country;
MODE = a dummy for foreign entry mode;
*KH*1 = know-how intensity measured by R&D spending as a percentage of sales;
*KH*2 = advertising spending as a percentage of sales;
*KH*3 = the sum of R&D and advertising as a percentage of sales.
On a two-tailed test, *Significant at 10% level, *Significant at 5% level, and ***Significant at 1% level.

valuation effect of FDI announcements should be explained by reasons other than the foreign earnings prospect.

The β_2 coefficient on *DIV* is positive and significant at the 5% level on a two-tailed *t*-test. Thus a firm's entry in a market in which it has no previous existence has a positive effect on its stock price, probably reflecting the diversification gain from foreign expansion. An insignificant β_3 indicates that the FDI valuation effect does not stem from the regional economics of target countries. An insignificant β_4 further shows the irrelevance of *MODE* in the model, and the market thus does not distinguish between a foreign entry by a greenfield project and a foreign entry through acquiring an existing unit.

Finally, the regression coefficient on know-how intensity is found to have different levels of significance with different proxies applied. In the second and fourth columns of Table 7.4, where both R&D and advertising variables are included as proxies for *KH*, the coefficient on the R&D variable is positive and significant at the 5% level. This suggests that only R&D intensive firms experience more positive abnormal returns at FDI announcements. However, because the R&D and advertising variables are highly correlated (correlation = 0.23), the coefficient estimates for these two variables are imprecise and erratic. The insignificance of the advertising variable is possibly due to the multicollinearity presented in the regression model. Thus *KH*3, the sum of R&D and advertising, is used as a proxy for know-how intensity, and the results are reported in columns one and three. The regression coefficient on *KH*3 is found to have a greater *t*-value, and the model also explains more variance than the case with only *KH*1 being included as a know-how proxy. This indicates that advertising spending has a certain explanatory power for the variation of abnormal returns across firms. In general, the results show that firms with a higher level of know-how intensity experience more positive cumulative abnormal returns on the event day.

In summary, the results of regression analysis show that MNEs with higher levels of know-how intensity have more positive value gains at FDI announcements. Furthermore, with *EFE* being included as a control variable, the relationship between know-how intensity and the FDI valuation effect should not be explained by the expected earnings effects of foreign expansion. The tests, therefore, conclude hypothesis H3c that the value increases experienced by know-how-intensive firms in the event period does not represent an incremental value associated with the expected performance of its assets to be employed overseas but reflects a revaluation of the firm's overall assets. While this valuation effect is positively related to know-how intensity, it may stem from the adjustment of the market price of a firm's intangible assets. The evidence supports the hypothesized information content of FDI announcements, suggesting that the FDI action conveys information about a firm's know-how and affects the valuation of its intangible assets. The results also show the existence of diversification benefits from the firm's FDI expansion.

SUMMARY

We have applied the event study method to examine stock price behavior in the period when an MNE makes a public announcement about its foreign investment. Our findings suggest that firms with a higher level of know-how intensity experience significant price appreciations at FDI announcements. The question remaining to be asked is whether the FDI valuation effect is attributed to the expected future foreign earnings or reflects additional information about the firm's know-how intangibles. Consequently, a cross-sectional regression analysis was performed to identify the sources of the FDI valuation effect. The results show a positive, significant relationship between the FDI valuation effect and know-how intensity, with the proxies for the expected foreign earnings and other economic variables included as control variables. The evidence suggests that the valuation effect of FDI announcements is not attributed to the expected earnings increase resulting from the planned foreign expansion. Instead, it represents a correction for the price of intangible assets based on information revealed by FDI announcements.

In conclusion, the market valuation study generates evidence confirming the thesis of FDI signaling, suggesting that foreign investment by an MNE is a market signal conveying information about firm-specific, know-how intangible assets. The findings are consistent with results in Chapter 6 based on the MNE's performance in product markets. However, since the event study method can clearly identify the cause-and-effect relationship between FDI and the market response, it provides more conclusive evidence in support of the FDI signaling theory.

NOTES

1. There is a lack of uniformity in accounting procedures because of the leeway a firm is permitted in its accounting treatments. Thus accounting profit may not reflect the firm's true foreign performance. Furthermore, the reported foreign earnings are subject to transfer price manipulation. Although such manipulation is outlawed by both host and home country governments, the MNE may employ it to achieve global optimization. Therefore, the measurement error could be a problem. We should be aware of the limitations of this proxy. However, this manipulation

may only increase the noise of data but not lead to a biased result (that could happen only if the distortion of foreign earnings is systematically associated with the know-how proxy, but there is no evidence to suggest such a pattern).

2. This study has further applied cross-sectional regression analysis to determine the relationship between the firm's foreign earnings performance *FEP* and its know-how intensity *KH* with size and other variables being controlled, where *FEP* is alternatively estimated by the ratio of foreign operation income to foreign sales and that to foreign assets and *KH* is estimated by annual R&D and advertising expenses as percentages of total sales. The results show that the regression coefficients on know-how proxies are significantly greater than zero, suggesting that the know-how intensive firms have superior foreign earnings performance. The results are based on a study of 746 firms, which represent all the U.S. public corporations that reported foreign operations and have no missing data in the 1977–88 period. The source of data is the VALU Line database.

8

Theory of Multinational Enterprises: Summary, Evaluation, and Future Directions

The major purpose of this book is to rectify the empirical deficiency of the internalization theory, a theory that has been widely considered a general explanation of multinational enterprises. We take a positivist economic approach, maintaining that the empirical nature of theories is a major basis for theory selection, and seek to develop an "auxiliary hypothesis" to enhance the empirical content of internalization. This approach leads to research on signaling effects of foreign direct investment, which also represents the first effort to apply signaling economics to study the FDI issue. In this framework, the internalization hypothesis can be tested indirectly, and the empirical investigation produces preliminary results. This final chapter concludes with a summary of the FDI signalling theory and major findings, which is followed by a critical assessment of this theory based on its contribution, limitations and policy implications, and a perspective on future research.

SUMMARY OF THE THEORY AND FINDINGS

Contemporary research has inherited a neoclassical economic framework, which justifies the multinational enterprise and its foreign investment based on the market imperfections paradigm. In the mainstream literature, market power and internalization are presented as two alternative approaches. The market power approach is developed in the industrial organization framework and views direct investment as a strategic action by an oligopolistic firm to take advantage of structural market imperfections and enhance its market power. On the other hand, the internalization approach is based on the transaction cost paradigm, which considers FDI an economic solution to obstacles in the transactional market and as a means to internalize transactions for efficiency gains. Both theories, judged by their explanatory power, are effective and can well explain the rise of the MNE institution and its foreign expansion. In the last two decades, however, there is an overwhelming shift of research from the market power approach to the internalization approach. Despite this trend, there is a need for an objective assessment of the literature on multinational enterprises.

According to a positive economic view, a theory is to explain and predict the economic phenomena, and it should be judged by whether and to what extent it can be confronted by the observable facts (i.e., refutable by evidence). Furthermore, since the research on multinational enterprises and direct investment has a strong positivist tradition, it is appropriate for us to evaluate different schools of thoughts by their respective empirical accomplishments. An overall review of the literature suggests that the industrial organization approach generates more convincing evidence in support of the market power hypothesis. In contrast, the empirical internalization research still fails to develop a framework to differentiate the theory from alternative hypotheses. Therefore, industrial organization performs better than internalization in terms of testability. This is at odds with the recent popularization of internalization. Can this be another case confirming McCloskey's view (1983) that in economics it is rhetoric that persuades economists? Alternatively, does it indicate that the selection of theory is made to serve the social need in response to global environmental changes (or mere reflect a renewed attitude toward multinational enterprises) rather than based on a value-free assessment of the theories?

However, we need to exercise caution in the assessment of research at this stage. While the empirical stagnation of internalization may represent a "degenerating problemshift," it is mainly due to low empirical content rather than the failure of the theoretical framework. Consequently, Buckley (1988) called it an urgent task to improve the empiricalness of internalization, and his proposed solution is to formulate some special theories and thus subject the theory to indirect tests. That is the direction taken by this book, and it leads to the construction of the FDI signaling framework. This framework has its theoretical foundation on the internalization theory, which rationalizes FDI by recognizing the obstacle to market transactions, particularly that due to imperfect information in the market. The signaling literature further suggests that market signaling should play a role in the market with asymmetric information. A synthesis of internalization and signaling theories provides a conceptual basis to explore the signaling issue associated with MNEs' operations. The elements required for a signaling equilibrium are derived from the FDI literature, and a framework of FDI signaling is constructed, and their implications are explored. The essential thesis is that the firm's FDI action has information content and affects the perception of less-informed market participants. Although the original purpose of FDI internalization is to internalize know-how transactions, this action may further convey information to the market with asymmetric information. FDI signaling provides guidance to examine the market consequences of the MNE's foreign investment.

The FDI signaling proposition has empirical implications and thus enables us to test the theory in the context of the MNE's product markets and capital markets. The results suggest (1) multinationals' FDI is positively associated with direct exports, and this effect is greater in magnitude for firms with higher levels of know-how intensity; (2) multinationals' FDI action is unrelated to their licensing sales for the whole sample, but the relationship becomes positively more significant for firms with higher levels of know-how intensity; and (3) multinationals' FDI announcements on average have no significant effect on the firm value, but the value impact will be positively significant for firms with higher levels of know-how intensity, and this valuation effect remains when the expected future foreign earnings and other operational effects are being controlled. Overall, these findings are consistent with the hypothesized information content of foreign direct investment, and the study thus confirms the FDI signaling proposition. It suggests that the firm's FDI action conveys information about its know-how-based intangible assets, thus promoting its market transactions and enhancing the value of its intangible assets.

Since the FDI signaling proposition is derived from the internalization theory, the test of the FDI signaling effect is a joint test of the FDI signaling proposition and the internalization hypothesis. In other words, the FDI signaling effect can exist only if the internalization hypothesis is valid. As such, a rejection of the FDI signaling proposition does not necessarily lead to a rejection of the internalization hypothesis, but a confirmation of the proposition should result in an acceptance of the internalization hypothesis. Since this investigation confirms the FDI signaling proposition, it also supports the internalization theory.

EVALUATION OF FDI SIGNALING RESEARCH

The outcome of a firm's multinationalization is a function of many variables. It is not the intention of this book to present FDI signaling as a new MNE theory or consider it as another explanation of foreign direct investment. We only postulate that the FDI signaling consequence may exist in the market, since the literature rationalizes FDI in a way which also satisfies the required signaling conditions specified by the signaling theory. Possibly, the FDI signaling effect comes out merely as a byproduct of the firm's foreign expansion through internalization.   A recognition of the signaling effect, however, gives rise to significant implications.   The significance of FDI signaling lies in its empiricalness.   It not only generates testable hypotheses, but also allows the test to be constructed as a joint test of FDI signaling and internalization propositions.   Consequently, it enhances empirical content of internalization and rectifies its "irrefutability," a major deficiency of that theory.   Furthermore, the FDI signaling theory explains some firms' peculiar FDI behavior, provides rich interpretations on the relations between MNEs' internalization and externalization, and presents implications on the social consequence of the firm's FDI expansion.

Contributions

The FDI signaling theory provides a framework with which to examine the interrelation between an MNE's internalization and externalization.   If the FDI signaling effect exists, a firm's establishment in foreign markets can promote its name recognition.   Consequently, FDI internalization, as advertisement and other kinds of market promotion, will positively affect the firm's market transactions (e.g., a parent firm's investment in a foreign country may promote its direct exports and licensing sales there).   The FDI action can be a credible signal to promote the firm's markets further because it cannot be mimicked by all other firms (which is a required condition for Spence-type signaling).   Thus the theory predicts a complementary relationship between FDI and trade, and between FDI and licensing.   Based on the cognitive implications, therefore, a link can be established between MNEs' internalization and externalization.

The theory advances our understanding of certain aspects of MNEs' behavior.   It not only presents additional explanation to the firm's interest to expand internationally but also rationalizes its apparent eagerness to boast of its MNE status.   For example, it explains the fact that many U.S. public corporations pursue voluntary foreign disclosure and reveal their foreign operation results to an extent well beyond the regulatory requirement (which is contradictory to the common belief that corporate America generally resists pressure for additional public disclosure).   In addition, it provides an explanation for some FDI phenomena that cannot be adequately explained by economic rationale, such as major U.S. accounting firms' early entry into China's market.   The behavior, however, can be easily understood in the context of FDI signaling.   With the additional gain associated with the perceptual effect of FDI, the firms have an incentive to publicize their foreign presence.   This incentive may further motivate them to expand foreign investment more aggressively, to a level that may be perceived as overextended abroad in the existing paradigm.

The FDI signaling framework further provides an interactive setting to explore the firm's internalization. It suggests that the firm's FDI action affects other market participants' perceptions and behavior and that the anticipation of such effects in turn may further affect the firm's behavior. Therefore, the FDI signaling research adds a dynamic element into internalization, which in the neoclassical framework is static in nature. Furthermore, if the firm recognizes the gains associated with FDI signaling, it will be more willing to choose FDI as a strategy for international expansion. In pursuing this expansion, the firm will adopt an integrated approach—it will not only evaluate the operational costs and benefits associated with an FDI option but also consider the perceptual impact of the internalization action (namely, the FDI signaling effect). In other words, the firm will seek, instead of a piecemeal approach, the maximization of overall gains from various forms of foreign involvements. This approach overcomes the limitation of the transaction-cost-based internalization paradigm, which assumes that the firm economizes the cost of transactions on an individual basis and pursues separate optimization. This study thus leads to a more balanced approach to MNEs' internalization and externalization.

Most importantly, this book enhances the explanatory power of the internalization theory, and improves its empiricalness and thus scientific nature. The FDI signaling framework provides an additional explanation for MNEs' behavior. This explanation, however, does not rely on the formulation of a new theory but is derived from the internalization theory. Thus, the explanatory power of FDI signaling belongs to the internalization theory. Internalization, despite its popularity, has suffered from its low empirical content, as no empirical design can be constructed as a true test of the internalization hypothesis. However, if a theory cannot be tested, then it is a tautology and its scientific nature can be questioned. Therefore, when the FDI signaling research presents a framework for a joint test of internalization, which can be in a rigorous fashion for the market-value-based test, it leads to enhance the empirical content of internalization. In short, this research promotes the "progressive problemshift" and is in the direction proposed by Buckley (1988).

Implications of FDI Signaling

The FDI signaling framework is relevant to the debate on the efficiency consequence of MNEs' operations. Hymer (1970) suggested that the major purpose of foreign direct investment is to remove competition. Sharing similar viewpoints, certain interest groups in both home and host countries cry out for more restrictions on MNEs. The subsequent literature (Casson

1987, Dunning and Rugman 1985, Rugman 1986, Teece 1985) has criticized Hymer for overemphasizing MNEs' market power and monopoly benefits and not considering that "the hierarchical organizational structure can replace imperfect markets for reasons of efficiency" (Dunning and Rugman 1985, p. 229). However, this view is primarily based on an ex ante approach. In fact the internalization theory as a whole gives little consideration to the market consequence of the firm's foreign investment. The impact of MNEs' operations on market structure, however, is important to the welfare analysis. For that matter, the FDI signaling research rectifies the weakness of internalization by providing it a conceptual framework for ex post analysis.

The FDI signaling theory provides an additional argument to support the efficiency consequence of MNEs' operations. With the existence of FDI signaling, the operations of the MNE institution may subsequently attenuate information asymmetry and thus improve the efficiency of the market. While evidence is produced to support FDI signaling, the efficiency-consequence argument is further strengthened. A major implication of FDI signaling to the operations of an international economy is that the firm's FDI expansion reduces market obstacles associated with cognitive imperfections and thus promotes the growth and efficiency of international markets.

The extended internalization theory (extended by the recognition of FDI signaling effects) has a prescriptive power in advancing our understanding of the multinational enterprise. Consequently, we not only view the MNE as an economic institution choosing alternatively between FDI and market modes for the maximum efficiency gain but also consider these two transactional modes as integral parts of the firm's activities to promote its internationalization. The implication is that FDI internalization is chosen for efficiency purposes, but this action may also have the effect in improving the external market conditions and thus promoting its market transactions. This approach helps rectify some popular misconceptions. In the height of FDI growth, concern was raised on the destructive effect of FDI expansion on international market transactions. While such a concern lacks empirical support, it now can also be refuted by the extended internalization theory. The view presented in this book is that FDI, with its consequence to alleviate market imperfections, will grow together with the market and promote both the firm's internalization and externalization.

Furthermore, it also rejects the view that internalization may have become obsolete (Michalet 1989). The question was raised mainly because MNEs in the 1970s are seen increasingly using various market modes to serve foreign markets. While this trend is noticed, it has been welcomed by some regulators and academia. According to this book, it should not be an issue whether FDI will eventually die out or not. FDI internalization and market modes are alternative devices chosen by the firm based on efficiency considerations. FDI has its merits and purpose when there are market imperfections. Moreover, given the effect of FDI to promote external market transactions, the firm may be more willing to pursue internalization at a multinational level. The important implication is that internalization and externalization are two aspects of an MNE's operations, which coexist and should not be considered mutually exclusive.

Intuitively, the internalization theory based on the FDI signaling framework provides a broad interpretation at the macro level. An MNE may undertake direct investment to enter a highly imperfect market, and this action in turn leads to reduction of imperfections and promoting the market growth. A good example may be China. At the time when it first opened the door to the outside world in 1978, the economy was essentially self-contained, with the structure distorted by over thirty years of central planning, operating under an outdated technology and management system, lacking the workable market mechanism, and conducting trade under numerous government restrictions such as high tariffs, quotas, import licenses, and foreign exchange controls. Given the existence of severe market imperfections, it was difficult, if not impossible, for many foreign firms to take advantage of the opportunity in China by trade. International exchange was unattractive despite the potential of that economy with its huge population, abundant resources, and cheap labor. Direct investment became a more preferred choice for foreign firms when this entry mode was allowed by the Chinese government. The foreign multinationals brought in capital, technology and market access critical for economic growth. Most importantly, these firms' operations promoted the development and improvement of the market mechanism. Today, this market is still highly imperfect, but with the private sector producing 53% of industrial output and trade representing over 30% of national economy, China is increasingly integrated into the global economy and is closer to a market economy than at any time in its history. The country (under pressure) is seen to adopt a series of measures to reduce tariff and non-tariff trade barriers, and the government has put it on agenda to make its currency *Renminbi* fully convertible in the near future. Apparently, FDI is one of the major factors which promote the reduction of market imperfections. As a result of FDI operations, the conditions for trade have been improved, and we may expect to see the shift of the weight of China's international economic activities from firms' internalization to more market-based transactions. The major point presented in this discussion is that FDI internalization, as some other mechanisms to countervail the market imperfections, is developed not only to substitute for the existing market but also to facilitate the market formation in a long run.

However, FDI signaling may add more to the controversy over the long-term effects of an MNE's operations on the home country economy. There are different views on the economic effects of the firm's expansion of foreign production in terms of its impact on domestic employment, capital formation, real income, and economic growth (Bergsten et al. 1978, Musgrave 1975). Certain groups propose restrictions on the firm's foreign expansion, believing that this investment has hurt domestic economic growth. The FDI signaling theory also has implications to this issue. With the existence of FDI signaling, an MNE may overinvest abroad in the sense that the firm's foreign investment is beyond the point at which marginal revenue equals marginal cost. However, the same theory further argues that such a strategy may stimulate the growth of the domestic market, with FDI signaling promoting the MNE's external market transactions, such as direct exports and licensing sales. Support for this contention is found in the statistics in Appendix B. However, with such complications, the overall effect becomes more difficult to determine.

Limitations

There are limitations in our study on the signaling effects of foreign direct investment. For example, one test was performed by examining the effect of MNEs' internalization on its externalization. Thus, regression models are developed with internalization proxies as independent variables and externalization proxies as dependent variables and with the inclusion of other control variables. While the results suggest a significantly positive relationship between these two types of variables, this study concludes that the expansion of the former may promote the growth of the latter as well. However, the regression method can only determine the existence of a statistical relationship between these two types of variables, but it is incapable of identifying which of these two is a causal variable. Therefore, this test per se has not verified the existence of such a cause-and-effect relationship between MNEs' internalization and externalization. It only supports the postulated relationship, which is entirely derived from the FDI signaling framework. To determine this cause-and-effect relationship, a more appropriate approach is the conventional event study method, which can establish a cause-and effect relationship based on examining the stock market response to the specific move of the firm.

Therefore, the event study method was further applied to investigate the effect of a firm's FDI announcement on its stock prices, with the price changes used as a measure of information content of FDI signaling. However, the valuation effect can be observed only if the FDI announce-ments are unexpected. The market generally has certain anticipations about a firm's foreign expansion. Depending on whether or to what extent the firm lives up to this anticipation, the market may respond to the FDI announcement in different ways. While this expectation is difficult to measure, we simply assume that the market's expectation of the firm's FDI expansion is zero. Clearly, such an assumption may not be valid, and the effect of this simplification is difficult to estimate. Furthermore, to eliminate the valuation effect attributed to the operational effects of FDI, we include empirical measures, such as the expected foreign earnings effects as control variables in the regression model. Here, our simple assumption is that the market believes that the firm's new foreign venture will have the same earnings performance as its previous foreign ventures. This proxy may result in measurement errors because the market could have better ways to estimate future foreign earnings. Again, the effect is difficult to estimate.

Another potential problem in the signaling test is associated with know-how proxies. Here the firm-specific know-how is broadly defined and includes the firm's proprietary knowledge, such as engineering expertise, process specifications, product design, and management and marketing skills. We use the firm's spending on R&D and advertising as proxies for intangible assets or the level of know-how intensity and sophistication. These proxies, however, only measure the technical aspects of know-how. Some other types of know-how (for example, management skills) are acquired through business operations rather than through spending on certain expense items and may not be captured in the study. Furthermore, although it is a common practice to estimate the firm's know-how intangible assets by its spending on R&D and advertising, there are limitations in using the input variables as proxies for the output measurements. Obviously, higher spending in R&D does not necessarily guarantee the creation of more valuable know-how intangibles. (Otherwise the market can determine a firm's know-how simply by its R&D or advertising spending level and there is no role for FDI signaling). Readers should be fully aware of these limitations when reading the study results.

FUTURE RESEARCH

This study represents a first step toward exploration of the FDI signaling effect. Recognition of this concept will increase the rigor and explanatory power of the internalization theory and provide a promising way to overcome the empirical obstacle of internalization. However, there is a need for substantially more work to refine the FDI signaling framework. From a theoretical standpoint, the signaling model should be further expanded, possibly by including the uncertainty factor or by developing a temporal model. The internalization theory may also be restructured by recognizing the FDI signaling effect, which may lead to a presentation of the framework in a more rigorous fashion. The empirical basis of the FDI signaling theory could be expanded. Although our preliminary study provides supportive findings, more empirical evidence needs to be gathered before acceptance of the FDI signaling proposition. Within the constraint of data availability, the FDI signaling proposition needs to be investigated more intensively, by measuring various effects of a firm's foreign expansion. For example, additional event studies can be performed with more effective control on the prospective FDI earnings and other possible sources of valuation effects. The FDI signaling effect may be also tested by examining its valuation effect on major competitors in the industries. Furthermore, the test may also be based on a firm's product markets by identifying those effects that cannot be explained by the operational effects of foreign direct investment. In short, the recognition of the FDI signaling enriches the literature and offers many promising areas of future research.

Appendix A
Definition of Terms and Concepts

The following terms are used throughout this book:

Barrier to Entry

It is the advantage that the established firms have over the potential entrants to the industry. Such advantages can be attributed to the absolute cost advantages enjoyed by existing firms, product differentiation, and economies of scale (Bain 1956), which determine the relative ease with which an outside firm enters the industry. The entry barrier is a determinant factor of industrial performance. Only when the barrier exists to a substantial extent can the firms in an industry enjoy sustained high profitability without inviting new competition. A modern version of the analysis of entry barriers can be found in Porter (1980). Based on Bain's analysis on the firm's strategic behavior to influence the entry barrier, Hymer (1976) further suggested that FDI is a conduct of oligopolistic firms to enhance the entry barrier.

Externalization

Opposite to internalization, externalization refers to the situation in which a firm engages in arm's length transactions to sell intermediate products, such as know-how and unfinished products, across countries.

Failure of the Market

It occurs when a specific transaction can be organized more efficiently within the firm (or by internalization) than through the market, given the obstacles to using the market.

FDI Signaling Effect

The action of foreign direct investment is proposed to have information content. A firm's FDI action may reveal certain unobservable features, such as the value of its intangible assets, and thus influence the perception and behavior of less informed buyers and investors in the market. As a result, the firm's FDI action may further affect its position in the product markets and its stock price in the securities market.

Foreign Direct Investment (FDI)

Hymer (1976) distinguished foreign direct investment from international capital movement, holding that FDI is a mechanism used by a multinational enterprise to maintain control over productive activities outside its national boundaries. More specifically, through the process of FDI, "the MNE transfers intermediate products such as knowledge or technology among its units across different nations while still retaining property rights over such assets" (Dunning and Rugman, 1985, p.228).

Information Asymmetry

Information asymmetry refers to the situation in which some market participants (insiders) have access to information that is not available to other market participants (outsiders). For example, a manager has more information than an investor about the profit prospects of the firm, a seller knows more than a buyer about the quality of its products, and a job applicant is more aware of his or her own productive ability than the potential employer.

Intangible Asset

The firm's intangible asset, distinguished from its assets in a tangible form such as land, building and machinery, is mainly knowledge-based. The intangible asset consists of proprietary know-how including quality control, engineering expertise, management and marketing skills, and trademarks and patented formulas and production processes (see Technological Know-how). While the firm's ownership of intangible assets secures it a competitive edge in the market and a stream of future cash flows, the market recognizes the firm's know-how advantage by pricing it at a value above total replacement costs of its tangible assets.

Internalization

A transaction is internalized when it is organized between parties under common ownership and with the price mechanism replaced by the hierarchial directive. This is the perspective that originated in Coase's theory of the firm (1937). The efficiency gain associated with internal transactions of knowledge-based products is further emphasized by the internalization theory as a major explanation for the rise of the MNE and its foreign investment (Buckley and Casson 1976). Thus, unless specified otherwise, in this text *internalization* refers to the internalization of transactions across national borders.

Market Signal

The role of market signaling arises in markets with asymmetric information. A market signal is an attribute or action adopted by some market participants (the more informed party), which, by design or accident, conveys information to other market participants (the less informed party) and alters their beliefs and perceptions (Spence 1974).

Market Structure

Market structure is the configuration of the market in which competing firms interact. It includes elements such as the number and size of firms in the market, the existence of economies of scale, and the extent of product differentiation, which all have a strategic influence on the nature of competition and pricing behavior. According to industrial organization economics, the structural feature of the market has a profound effect on industry performance as measured by profitability, growth, and technical progress, and it further determines the productive efficiency of the economy in terms of resources allocation and economic welfare.

Multinational Enterprise (MNE)

The MNE is defined as a firm that undertakes foreign direct investment. It has been conceptualized as "an organization that internalizes various international transactions which could conceivably take place in a market" (Teece 1981b, p. 3). Furthermore, an MNE chooses discriminatively, based on the efficiency consideration, between FDI internalization and market arrangements, which include exports, licensing, management contract and turnkey projects, for the entry mode by which to serve foreign markets. This book, in recognizing the FDI signalling effect, assumes that the MNE seeks to optimize overall operations of internalization and externalization activities.

Structural Market Imperfections

Structural market imperfections are certain features of market structure under which perfect competition yields to imperfect competition, ranging from monopolistic competition, to oligopoly, to monopoly. Market structure is highly imperfect when the market concentration is high (e.g., when the industry consists of a small number of large firms) and the entry barrier is significant (i.e., the established firms have substantial advantages over the new entrants attributed to the absolute cost advantage, product differentiation, and economies of scale). As a result, the leading firms enjoy considerable market power; that is, they have the ability to influence the market price perceptibly.

Technological Know-how

Technological know-how can be broadly defined as the stock of proprietary knowledge, patented or unpatented, created in a firm's research and development (R&D) activities and business operations. It mainly takes three different forms: hardware embodying know-how, such as machinery and equipment and turnkey projects; software, such as blueprints, formulas and process specifications; and services of technicians and professionals for quality improvement, engineering expertise, management and marketing skills, and process and product design. The software and service components of know-how have become increasingly important since the advent of information technology as the central element in the production methods of most goods and services (UNCTC 1988).

Transactional Market Imperfections

Transactional market imperfections stem from obstacles to organizing transactions through the market, which are attributed to the interface of cognitive deficiencies and specific environmental conditions. The cognitive deficiencies include the opportunistic human behavior and bounded rationality, and the environmental factors include uncertainty and the small number of market participants (Williamson 1975). The existence of these obstacles prevents the market from being an efficient means to achieve economic coordination and resource allocation.

Appendix B
Historical Data of the MNE's Operations

Table B.1

Distribution of Ownership Patterns of 1,276 Manufacturing Affiliates of 391 Multinational Enterprises Established in Developing Countries, 1951–75

Home countries and Type of Ownership	Number Established as Percentage of Total				
	Before 1951	1951–60	1961–65	1965–70	1971–75
Affiliates of 180 U.S.-based corporations					
Wholly owned (95% & above)	58.4	44.5	37.4	46.2	43.7
Majority owned (over 50%)	12.2	21.4	19.2	17.8	17.3
Co-owned (50:50)	5.6	7.9	11.4	11.2	10.4
Minority owned (5–50%)	11.2	18.8	21.7	21.5	28.1
Unknown	12.6	7.4	10.3	3.3	0.4
Total	100.0	100.0	100.0	100.0	100.0
Affiliates of 135 European (including UK) based corporations					
Wholly owned (95% & above)	39.1	31.6	20.9	18.9	
Majority owned (over 50%)	15.4	20.1	15.6	16.4	
Co-owned (50:50)	5.3	6.6	11.1	6.6	
Minority owned (5–50%)	9.8	27.9	35.8	42.1	
Unknown	30.5	13.9	16.6	16.0	
Total	100.0	100.0	100.0	100.0	n.a.
Affiliates of 76 other multinational enterprises					
Wholly-owned (95% and above)	27.4	16.7	10.7	6.1	
Majority-owned (over 50%)	8.2	26.2	12.6	8.2	
Co-owned (50:50)	12.3	7.1	6.3	7.5	
Minority-owned (5–50%)	16.4	42.9	66.7	74.2	
Unknown	35.6	7.1	3.8	3.9	
Total	100.0	100.0	100.0	100.0	n.a.

Source: UNCTC, *Transnational Corporations in World Development: Re-Examination* (1978). Used with permission.

Note: n.a. = not available.

Figure B.1
U.S. Receipts of Royalty and Licensing Fees

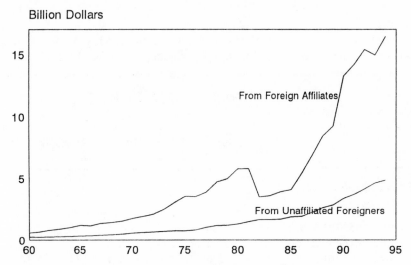

Sources: U.S. Department of Commerce, Bureau of Economic Analysis,
Current Survey of Business, various issues.

Figure B.2
U.S. Licensing Receipts from Developing Countries

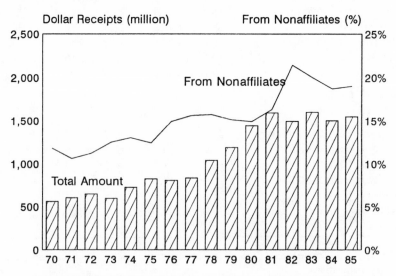

Sources: U.S. Department of Commerce, Bureau of Economic Analysis,
Survey of Business, various issues.

Appendix C
Explanation of the MERM Exchange Rate

The relative strength of a home currency may affect the competitiveness of a nation's industry and export business. In the empirical models of equations (6.2) and (6.4), to control the effect of exchange rate changes on the export variable, the nominal relative exchange rate is included as one independent variable.

The nominal effective exchange rate index represents the ratio of the period average exchange rate of one currency, here the U.S. dollar, to a weighted geometric average of exchange rates for the currencies of U.S. major trade partner countries. Here an appreciation of the U.S. dollar will be reflected as an increase of the index value. A number of measures of effective exchange rate are developed by the International Monetary Fund (IMF) Research Department. This book uses the nominal relative exchange rate index that is based on the weights derived from the IMF Multilateral Exchange Rate Model (MERM). The weights are estimated for 1977 and comprise trade and nontrade goods; they take into account the size and direction of trade flows in the base year as well as the relevant price elasticities and effects of exchange rate changes on domestic production. A complete discussion of the methodology is provided in Artus and McGuirk (1981).

The currency weights in the effective nominal dollar rate derived from the IMF's MERM are as follows:

Major Currency	Percentage weight
Australia (Dollar)	5.0
Austria (Schilling)	1.1
Britain (Pound)	5.2
Belgium (Franc)	2.4
Canada (Dollar)	20.7
Denmark (Krone)	1.4
France (Franc)	10.3
Germany (Mark)	13.2
Italy (Lira)	7.6
Japan (Yen)	21.7
Netherlands (Guilder)	3.3
Norway (Krone)	1.2
Spain (Peseta)	2.4
Sweden (Krona)	2.7
Switzerland (Franc)	1.7
Total	100.0

Appendix D
Major Industrial Groups
under the BEA Classification

Petroleum
    Oil and gas extraction
    Petroleum and coal products
    Petroleum wholesale trade
    Other

Manufacturing
    Food and kindred products
    Chemical and allied products
    Primary and fabricated metals
    Machinery, except electrical
    Electric and electronic equipment
    Transportation equipment
    Other manufacturing

Wholesale trade
    Durable goods
    Nondurable goods

Finance (except banking), insurance, and real estate
    Finance, except banking
    Insurance
    Real estate
    Holding companies

Services
    Hotel and other lodging places
    Business services
    Automotive rental and leasing, without drivers
    Motion pictures, including television tape and film
    Health services
    Engineering, architectural, and surveying services
    Management and public relation services
    Other services

Other industries
    Agriculture, forestry, and fishing
    Mining
    Construction transportation, communications, public utilities
    Retail trade

Source: The Department of Commerce, Bureau of Economic Analysis (1982).

Bibliography

Acharya, S. 1988. A generalized econometrics model and tests of a signalling hypothesis with two discrete signals. *Journal of Finance* (June): 413–429.

Agmon, T. and D. R. Lessard. 1977. Investor recognition of corporate international diversification. *Journal of Finance* 32 (September): 1049–55.

Aharoni, Yair. 1966. *The Foreign Direct Investment Process.* Boston, Mass.: Graduate School of Business Administration, Harvard University.

———. 1971. On the definition of a multinational corporation. *Quarterly Review of Economics and Business* 2, no. 3 (Autumn): 27–37.

Akerlof, George A. 1970. The market for 'lemons': Quality uncertainty and the market mechanism. *Quarterly Journal of Economics* (August): 488–500.

Aliber, Robert Z. 1970. A theory of foreign direct investment. In *The International Corporation,* edited by Kindleberger. Cambridge, Mass.: MIT Press, 17–34.

———. 1983. Money, Multinationals, and Sovereigns. In *The Multinational Corporation in the 1980s*, edited by C. P. Kindleberger and D. B. Audretsch. Cambridge, Mass.: MIT Press.

Anderson, Thomas, and Torbjörn Fredriksson. 1996. International organization of production and variation in exports from affiliates. *Journal of International Business Studies* 27, no. 2: 249–263.

Angel, Juvenal L. 1979. *Directory of American Firms Operating in Foreign Countries.* New York: Uniworld Business Publications.

Arrow, Kenneth J. 1962. Economic welfare and the allocation of resources for invention. In *The Rate and Direction of the Inventive Activity: Economic and Social Factors.* A report of the National Bureau of Economic Research. Princeton: Princeton University Press.

———. 1969. The organization of economic activity. *The Analysis and Evaluation of Public Expenditure: The PPB System.* Joint Economic Committee, 91st Cong., 1st Sess.: 59–73.

———. 1971. *Essays in the Theory of Risk Bearing.* Chicago: Markham.

Artus, Jacques and Anne McGuirk. 1981. A revised version of the multilateral exchange rate model. *IMF Staff Papers* 28 (June): 275–309.

Bain, Joe S. 1956. *Barriers to New Competition: Their Character and Consequences in Manufacturing Industries.* Cambridge: Harvard University Press.

———. 1959. *Industrial Organization.* New York: Wiley.

Ball, Ray, and P. Brown. 1968. An empirical evaluation of accounting income numbers. *Journal of Accounting Research* 6 (Autumn): 159–178.

Balvers, Ronald J., Bill McDonald, and Robert E. Miller. 1988. Underpricing of new issues and the choice of auditor as a signal of investment banker reputation. *Accounting Review* 63, no. 4 (October): 605–622.

Beaver, William H., Roger Clarke, and William R. Wright. 1979. The association between unsystematic security returns and the magnitude of earnings forecast errors. *Journal of Accounting Research* 17 (Autumn): 316–340.

Beaver, William H., and P. A. Griffin. 1980. The information content of SEC accounting series release No. 190. *Journal of Accounting and Economics* 2 (Autumn): 127–157.

Ben-Zion, Uri. 1984. The R&D and investment decision and its relationship to the firm's market value: Some preliminary results. In *R&D, Patents, and Productivity*, edited by Zvi Griliches. Chicago: University of Chicago Press.

Bergsten, C. F., T. Horst, and T. H. Moran. 1978. *American Multinationals and American Interests.* Washington, D.C.: Brookings Institution.

Blaug, Mark. 1976. Kuhn versus Lakatos or paradigms versus research programmes in the history of economics. *History of Political Economy* 7, no. 4 (Winter): 399–433.

Bond, Eric W. 1983. A direct test of the "lemons" model: The market for used pickup trucks. *The American Economic Review* (September): 836–840.

Buckley, Peter J. 1985. New forms of international industrial-cooperation. In *The Economic Theory of the Multinational Enterprise*, edited by Peter Buckley. New York: St. Martin's Press.

———. 1988. The limits of explanation: Testing the internalization theory of the multinational enterprise. *Journal of International Business Studies* 19 (Summer): 181–193.

———. 1989. Foreign market servicing strategies and competitiveness: A theoretical framework. In *International Strategic Management,* edited by Anant R. Negandhi and Arun Savara. Lexington, Mass.: Lexington Books.

Buckley, Peter J., and Michael Z. Brooke. 1992. *International Business Study: An Overview.* Cambridge, Mass.: Blackwell.

Buckley, Peter and Mark Casson. 1976. *The Future of the Multinational Enterprise.* New York: Holmes-Meier.

Calvet, A. Louis. 1981. A synthesis of foreign direct investment theories and theories of the multinational firm. *Journal of International Business Studies* (Spring/Summer): 43–59.

Casson, Mark. 1982. Transaction costs and the theory of the multinational enterprise. In *New Theory of the Multinational Enterprise*, edited by Alan Rugman. New York: St. Martin's Press.

———. 1987. *The Firm and the Market.* London: Basil Blackwell Ltd.

Caves, Richard E. 1964. *American Industry: Structure, Conduct, Performance.* Chicago: Prentice-Hall.

———. 1971. International corporations: The industrial economics of foreign investment. *Economica* 38 (February): 1–27.

———. 1974. Causes of direct investment: Foreign firms' shares in Canadian and United Kingdom manufacturing industries. *Review of Economics and Statistics* 56 (August): 279–293.

———. 1982. *Multinational Enterprise and Economic Analysis.* New York: Cambridge University Press.

Caves, Richard E., and Michael E. Porter. 1976. Barriers to exit. In *Essays on Industrial Organization in Honor of Joe Bain.* Cambridge, Mass.: Ballinger.

Caves, Richard E., Michael E. Porter, and A. M. Spence. 1980. *Competition in the Open Economy: A Model Applied to Canada.* Cambridge, Mass.: Harvard University Press.

Chang, Su Han, John D. Martin, and John W. Kensinger. 1990. Corporate research and development expenditures and share value. *Journal of Financial Economics* 26: 255–276.

Cho, Kang Rae. 1990. The role of product-specific factors in intra-firm trade of U.S. manufacturing multinational corporations. *Journal of International Business Studies* 21, no. 2: 319–330.

Clark, J. M. 1961. *Competition as a Dynamic Process.* Washington, D.C.: Brookings Institution.

Coase, Ronald. 1937. The nature of the firm. *Economica* 4 (November): 386–405.

Cockburn, Iain, and Zvi Griliches. 1987. Industry effects and appropriability measures in the stock market's valuation of R&D and patents. National Bureau of Economic Research, Working Paper Series no. 2465.

Cohen, Benjamin I. 1972. Foreign investment by U.S. corporations as a way of reducing Risk. Economic Growth Center Discussion Paper no. 151, Yale University.

Connor, J. M. 1977. *The Market Power of Multinationals: A Quantitative Analysis of U.S. Corporations in Brazil and Mexico.* New York: Praeger.

Contractor, Farok J. 1980. The profitability of technology licensing by U.S. multinationals: A framework for analysis and empirical study. *Journal of International Business Studies* 11 (Fall): 40–63.

———. 1981. *International Technology Licensing: Compensation, Costs, and Negotiation.* Lexington, Mass.: Lexington Books.

———. 1985. Licensing Versus Foreign Direct Investment in U.S. Corporate Strategy: An Analysis of Aggregate U.S. Data. In *International Technology Transfer: Concepts, Measures, and Comparison,* edited by Nathan Rosenberg and Claudio Frischtak. New York: Praeger.

Contractor, Farok J., and Tagi Safafi-nejad. 1981. International technology transfer: Major issues and policy responses. *Journal of International Business Studies* (Fall): 113–135.

Deane, R. S. 1970. *Foreign Investment in New Zealand Manufacturing.* Wellington, New Zealand: Sweet and Maxwell.

Denekamp, Johannes G. 1995. Intangible assets, internalization and foreign direct investment in manufacturing. *Journal of International Business Studies* 26, no. 3: 493–504.

Dewenter, Kathryn L. 1995. Are intra-industry investment patterns consistent with cost disadvantages to cross-border investing? Evidence from the U.S. chemistry industry. *Journal of International Business Studies* 26, no. 4: 843–857.

Doukas, John, and Nickolaos G. Travlos. 1988. The effect of corporate multinationalism on shareholders' wealth: Evidence from international acquisition. *Journal of Finance* 23: 1161–75.

Drucker, Peter F. 1972. *Concept of the Corporation.* New York: John Day Co.

Dunning, John. 1958. *American Investment in British Manufacturing Industry.* London: Allen & Unwin.

———. 1973. The determinants of international production. *Oxford Economic Papers* 25, no. 3: 289–336.

———. 1979. Explaining changing patterns of international production: In defence of the eclectic theory. *Oxford Bulletin of Economics and Statistics* (February): 269-291.

———. 1981. *International Production and the Multinational Enterprise.* London: Unwin.

———. 1988. *Explaining International Production.* London: Unwin Hyman.

Dunning, John, and Alan Rugman. 1985. In honor of Stephen H. Hymer: The first quarter century of the theory of foreign direct investment. *The American Economic Review* 75 (May): 228–232.

Eastman, H. C., and S. Stykolt. 1967. *The Tariff and Competition in Canada.* Toronto: Macmillan.

Errunza V. R., and L. W. Senbet. 1984. International corporate diversification, market valuation, and size-adjusted evidence. *Journal of Finance* 39 (July): 727–743.

———. 1981. The effects of international operations on the market value of the firm: Theory and evidence. *Journal of Finance* 36 (May): 401–417.

Fama, E. 1976. *Foundation in Finance.* New York: Basic Books.

Fatemi, Ali M. 1984. Shareholder benefits from corporate international diversification. *Journal of Finance* 39 (December): 1325-1343.

Financial Accounting Standard Board. 1976. *Statement of Financial Accounting Standards (SFAS) No. 14, Financial reporting for segments of a business enterprise.* Stamford, Conn.: Financial Accounting Standard Board.

———. 1974. *Statement of Financial Accounting Standards (SFAS) No. 2, Accounting for Research and Development.* Stamford, Conn.: Financial Accounting Standard Board.

Fishwick, F. 1981. *Multinational Companies and Economic Concentration in Europe.* Report submitted to Institute for Research and Information on Multinationals. Paris.

Flowers, Edward B. 1976. Oligopolistic reactions in European and Canadian direct investment in the United States. *Journal of International Business Studies* (Fall/Winter): 43–55.

Foster, George. 1975. Earnings and stock prices of insurance companies. *Accounting Review* 50 (October): 686–698.

Friedman, Milton. 1953. The methodology of positive economics. In *Essays in Positive Economics.* Chicago: University of Chicago Press.

Gaspari, K. Celeste. 1983. Foreign market operations and domestic market power. In *The Multinational Corporation in the 1980s*, edited by C. P. Kindleberger and D. B. Audretsch. Cambridge, Mass.: MIT Press.

Grant, Edward B. 1980. Market implications of differential amounts of interim information. *Journal of Accounting Research* 18 (Spring): 255-268.

Griliches, Zvi. 1981. Market value, R and D, and patents. *Economic Letters* 7: 183-187.

Grosse, Robert E. 1985. An imperfect competition theory of the MNE. *Journal of International Business Studies* 16: 37-56.

Grossman, S. J. 1981. The informational role of warranties and private disclosure about product quality. *Journal of Law and Economics* 24: 461-483.

Gruber, William, Dileep Mehta, and Raymond Vernon. 1967. The R&D factor in international trade and international investment of I. S. industries. *Journal of Political Economy* (February): 20-37.

Habermas, Jürgen. 1972. *Knowledge and Human Interests*. London: Heineman.

Harris, Robert S. and David Ravenscraft. 1991. The role of acquisitions in foreign direct investment: Evidence form the U.S. stock market. *Journal of Finance* 26, no. 3: 825-845.

Heflebower, Richard B. 1954. Toward a theory of industrial markets and prices. *American Economic Review* (May): 121-139.

Heil, Oliver, and Thomas S. Robertson. 1991. Toward a theory of competitive market signalling: A research agenda. *Strategic Management Journal* 12: 403-418.

Helleiner, G. K. 1973. Manufactured exports from less developed countries and multinational firms. *Economic Journal* (March): 21-47.

Helleiner, G. K., and R. Lavergne. 1979. Intra-firm trade and industrial exports to the United States. *Oxford Bulletin of Economics and Statistics* 41 (November): 297-311.

Hennart, Jean-François. 1982. *A Theory of Multinational Enterprise*. Ann Arbor, Michigan: University of Michigan Press.

———. 1991. The transaction costs theory of joint ventures: An empirical study of Japanese subsidiaries in the United States. *Management Science* 37 (April) 4: 483-493.

Hirsch, S. 1976. An international trade and investment theory of the firm. *Oxford Economic Papers* (July): 258-270.

Hirschey, Mark. 1981. R&D intensity and multinational involvement. *Economics Letters* 7, no. 1: 87-93.

———. 1982a. Market power and foreign Involvement by U.S. multinationals. *The Review of Economics and Statistics* 64, no. 2 (May): 343-345.

———. 1982b. Intangible capital aspects of advertising and R and D expenditures. *Journal of Industrial Economics* 30: 375-390.

Hood, Neil, and Stephen Young. 1979. *The Economics of Multinational Enterprise*. New York: Longman.

Horaguchi, Haruo, and Brian Toyne. 1990. Setting the record straight: Hymer, internalization theory and transaction cost economics. *Journal of International Business Studies* 21, no. 3: 487-494.

Horst, Thomas. 1971. The theory of the multinational firm: Optimal behavior under different tariff and tax rates. *Journal of Political Economy* 79 (September/October): 1059–1072.

———. 1972a. Firms and industry determinants of the decision to invest abroad: An empirical study. *The Review of Economic and Statistics*. (August): 258–266.

———. 1972b. The industrial composition of U.S. exports and subsidiary sales to the Canadian market. *American Economic Review* 62 (March): 37–45.

Horstmann, Ignatius, and James Markusen. 1987. Licensing versus direct investment: A model of internalization by the multinational enterprise. *Canadian Journal of Economics* (August): 464–481.

Hughes, P. 1986. Signalling by direct disclosure under asymmetric information. *Journal of Accounting and Economics* 8: 119–142.

Hymer, Stephen. 1968. La grande "corporation" multinationale: Analyse de certaines raison qui poussent a l'integration international des affaires. *Revue Economique* 14, no. 6: 949–973. Quoted in Horaguchi, Haruo and Brian Toyne, Setting the record straight: Hymer, internalization theory and transaction cost economics. *Journal of International Business Studies* 21 (1990): 487-494.

———. 1976. *The International Operations of National Firms: A Study of Direct Foreign Investment*. Cambridge, Mass.: MIT Press. Previously unpublished doctoral dissertation (MIT, 1960).

———. 1979. *The Multinational Corporation: A Radical Approach*. London: Cambridge University Press.

Ippolito, Pauline M. 1990. Bonding and nonbonding signals of product quality. *Journal of Business* 63: 41–60.

Itaki, Masahiko. 1991. A critical assessment of the eclectic theory of the multinational enterprise. *Journal of International Business Studies* 22, no. 3:445–460.

Jacquillat, B., and B. H. Solnik. 1978. Multinationals are poor tools for diversification. *Journal of Portfolio Management* 4 (November): 8–12.

Johnson, Harry. 1970. The Efficiency and Welfare Implications of International Corporation. In *International Corporation*, edited by Charles P. Kindleberger. Cambridge, Mass.: MIT Press.

Kang, Jun-Koo. 1993. The International market for corporate control. *Journal of Financial Economics* 34: 345–371.

Kay, Neil. 1983. Multinational enterprises: A review article. *Scottish Journal of Political Economy* 30 (November): 305–311.

Kemp, M. C. 1964. *The Pure Theory of International Trade*. Englewood Cliffs, N.J.: Prentice-Hall.

Keynes, John M. 1890. *The Scope of Methods of Political Economy*. London: Macmillan.

Kim, Wi Saeng, and Esmeralda O. Lyn. 1986. Excess market value, the multinational corporation, and Tobin's q-ratio. *Journal of International Business Studies* 17, no. 1 (Spring): 119–125.

Kindleberger, Charles P. 1969. *American Business Abroad: Six Lectures on Direct Investment*. New Haven, Conn.: Yale University Press.

———. 1984. *Multinational Excursions*. Cambridge, Mass.: MIT Press.

Knickerbocker, Frederick T. 1973. *Oligopolistic Reaction and Multinational Enterprise*. Boston, Mass.: Division of Research, Graduate School of Business Administration, Harvard University.

Kogut, Bruce. 1983. Foreign direct investment as a sequential process. In *The Multinational Corporations in 1980s,* edited by C. P. Kindleberger and D. Andretsch. Cambridge, Mass.: MIT Press.

Kogut, Bruce, and Udo Zander. 1993. Knowledge of the firm and the evolutionary theory of the multinational corporation. *Journal of International Business Studies* 24, no. 4: 625–645.

Kojima, Kiyoshi. 1978. *Direct Foreign Investment: A Japanese Model of Multinational Business Operations*. London: Croom Helm.

Kuhn, Thomas S. 1962. *The Structure of Scientific Revolutions*. Chicago: University of Chicago Press.

———. 1970. Logic of discovery or psychology of research? In *Criticism and the Growth of Knowledge,* edited by Imre Lakatos and Alan Musgrave. New York: Cambridge University Press.

Lakatos, Imre. 1970. Falsification and the methodology of scientific research programmes. In *Criticism and the Growth of Knowledge,* edited by Imre Lakatos and Alan Musgrave. London: Cambridge University Press.

———. 1974. Science and pseudoscience. *Conceptus* 8: 5–9.

Lall, Sanjaya. 1979. Multinationals and market structure in an open developing economy: The case of Malaysia. *Weltwirtschaftliches Archiv* 115, no. 5: 325–335.

———. 1981. The pattern of intra-firm exports by U.S. multinationals. *Oxford Bulletin of Economics and Statistics* (November): 283–307.

Lall, Sanjaya, and N. S. Siddharthan. 1982. The monopolistic advantages of multinationals: Lessons from form foreign direct investment in the U.S. *The Economic Journal* 92: 668–683.

Lee, Kwang, and Chuck Kwok. 1988. Multinational corporations vs. domestic corporations: International environment factors and determinants of capital structure. *Journal of International Business Studies* (Summer): 195–217.

Leland, Hayne E., and David H. Pyle. 1977. Information asymmetries, financial structure, and financial intermediation. *Journal of Finance* (May): 371–387.

Lindenberg, R.B., and S. A. Ross. 1981. Tobin's q Ratio and Industrial Organization. *Journal of Business* 54, no. 1: 1–32.

Lipsey, Robert, and Merle Weiss. 1981. Foreign production and exports in manufacturing industries. *The Review of Economics and Statistics* (November): 488–494.

———. 1984. Foreign production and exports of individual firms. *The Review of Economics and Statistics* (May): 304–308.

MacDougall, G. D. 1960. The benefits and costs of private investment abroad: A theoretical approach. *Economic Record* 36 (March): 13–35.

Magee, Stephen. 1977. Information and the multinational corporation: An appropriability theory of foreign direct investment. In *The New International Economic Order: The North-South Debate*, edited by Jagdish Bhagati. Cambridge, Mass.: MIT Press, Bicentennial Studies.

Markusen, James R. 1984. Multinationals, multi-plant economies, and the gains from trade. *Journal of International Economics* 6: 205–226.

Mason, Edward S. 1939. Price and production policies of large-scale enterprise. *American Economic Review*, Supplement (March): 61–74.

Mason, R. H. 1980. A comment on professor Kojima's Japanese type versus American type of technology transfer. *Hitosubashi Journal of Economics* 20: 242–252.

McClain, D. 1983. Foreign direct investment in the United States: Old currents, "new waves," and the theory of direct investment. In *The Multinational Corporation in the 1980s*, edited by C. P. Kindleberger and D. B. Audretsch. Cambridge, Mass.: MIT Press.

McCloskey, D. 1983. The rhetoric of economics. *Journal of Economic Literature* 21: 481–516.

McManus, J. C. 1972. The theory of the international firm. In *The Multinational Firm and the Nation State,* edited by G. Paquet. Toronto: Collier Macmillan.

Meade, J. E. 1971. *The Controlled Economy*. London: Allen & Unwin.

Michalet, Charles-Albert. 1989. The internalization concept revisited. *The CTC Reporter* 28 (Autumn): 62–64.

Miller, Merton, and Kevin Rock. 1985. Dividend policy under asymmetric information. *The Journal of Finance* (September): 1031–1051.

Modigliani, Franco, and Merton H. Miller. 1958. The cost of capital, corporation finance and the theory of investment. *American Economic Review* (June): 261–297.

Morch, Randall, and Bernard Yeung. 1991. Why investors value multinationality. *Journal of Business* 64: 165–187.

———. 1992. Internalization: An event study test. *Journal of International Economics* 33: 41–56.

Morley, Samuel A., and Gordon W. Smith. 1971. Import substitution and foreign investment in Brazil. *Oxford Economic Paper* (March): 120–135.

Muller, D. C., and J. E. Tilton. 1969. Research and development costs as a barrier to entry. *Canadian Journal of Economics* 2 (November): 570–579.

Musgrave, Peggy B. 1975. *Direct Investment Abroad and the Multinationals: Effects on the United States Economy*. Washington, D.C.: U.S. Government Printing Office.

Myers, S. C., and N. S. Majluf. 1984. Corporate financing and investment decision when firms have information that investors do not have. *Journal of Financial Economics* 13:187–221.

National Register Publishing Co. 1980. *International Directory of Corporate Affiliations*. Skokie, Ill.: Macmillan.

OECD. 1987. *International Technology Licensing: Survey Results*. May (mimeographed).

Olin, Bertile. 1933. *Interregional and International Trade*. Cambridge, Mass.: Harvard University Press.

Oman, Charles. 1984. *New Forms of International Investment in Developing Countries*. Paris: OECD Development Center.

Pakes, Ariel. 1985. On patents, R and D, and the stock market rate of return. *Journal of Political Economy* 93: 390–409.

Parker, J. 1974. *The Economics of Innovation: The National and International Enterprise in Technology Change.* London: Longman.

Parry, T. G. 1978. Structure and performance in Australian manufacturing: With special reference to foreign-owned enterprise. In *Growth, Trade and Structural Change in an Open Australian Economy,* edited by W. Kasper and T. G. Parry. Kensington, Australia: Center for Applied Economic Research, University of New South Wales.

Patell, James M. 1976. Corporate forecasts of earnings per share and stock price behavior: Empirical tests. *Journal of Accounting Research* 14 (August): 247–276.

Popper, Karl R. 1959. *The Logic of Scientific Discovery.* New York: Harper Torchbooks.

Porter, Michael E. 1980. *Competitive Strategy: Techniques for Analyzing Industries and Competitors.* New York: Free Press.

Pugel, T. A. 1978. *International Market Linkages and U.S. Manufacturing: Prices, Profits and Patterns.* Cambridge, Mass.: Ballinger.

Riedel, James. 1975. The nature and determinants of export-oriented direct foreign investment in a developing country: A case study of Taiwan. *Weltwirtschaftliches Archiv* 111: 505–528.

Riley, John G. 1979. Informational Equilibrium. *Econometrica* 47, no. 2 (March): 331–359.

Ross, Stephen A. 1977. The determination of financial structure: The incentive signalling approach. *Bell Journal of Economics and Management Science* 8 (Spring): 23–40.

Rothschild, M., and J. Stiglitz. 1976. Equilibrium in competitive insurance markets: An essay on the economics of imperfect information. *Quarterly Journal of Economics* 90: 629–649.

Rugman, Alan M. 1976. Risk Reduction by International Diversification. *Journal of International Business Studies* (Fall/Winter): 75–80.

———. 1979. *International Diversification and the Multinational Enterprise.* Lexington, Mass.: D.C. Health.

———. 1980. Internalization as a general theory of foreign direct investment: A reappraisal of the literature. *Weltwirstschaftliches Archiv* 116, no. 2: 365–379.

———. 1981. *Inside the Multinationals: The Economics of Internal Markets.* London: Croom Helm.

———. ed. 1982. *New Theory of Multinational Enterprise.* New York: St. Martin's Press.

———. 1986. New theories of the multinational enterprise: An assessment of internalization theory. *Bulletin of Economic Research* 38, no. 2: 101–118.

Salinger, M. 1981. *Tobin's q, Investment, and Monopoly Power.* Cambridge, mimeo.

Sawyer, Malcolm C. 1981. *The Economics of Industries and Firms: Theories, Evidence and Policy.* Surry Hills, Australia: Croom Helm.

Scherer, Frederic M. 1970. *Industrial Market Structure and Economic Performance.* Chicago: Rand McNally.

Scherer, Frederic M., and David R. Ross. 1990. *Industrial Market Structure and Economic Performance.* 3rd ed. Boston, Mass.: Houghton Mifflin.

Senchack, A. J., and W. L. Beedles. 1980. Is direct international diversification desirable? *Journal of Portfolio Management* 6 (Winter): 49–57.

Shapiro, Daniel M. 1983. Entry, exit and the theory of the multinational corporation. In *The Multinational Corporation in the 1980s,* edited by C. P. Kindleberger and D. B. Audretsch. Cambridge, Mass.: MIT Press.

Simon, Herbert A. 1979. Rational decision making in business organizations. *American Economic Review* 69, no. 4 (September): 493–519.

Sosnick, Steven H. 1958. A critique of concepts of workable competition. *Quarterly Journal of Economics* (August): 416–423.

Spence, Michael. 1973. Job market signaling. *Quarterly Journal of Economics* 87 (August): 355–379.

———. 1974. *Market Signaling: Information Transfer in Hiring and Related Screening Processes.* Cambridge, Mass.: Harvard University Press.

———. 1976. Informational aspects of market structure: An introduction. *Quarterly Journal of Economics* 90 (November): 591–597.

———. 1977. Consumer misperception, product failure, and product liability. *Review of Economic Studies* 44, no. 3: 561–572.

Steuer, M. D. et al. 1973. *The Impact of Foreign Direct Investment on the United Kingdom.* London: Her Majesty's Stationery Office.

Stopford, John. 1982. *The World Directory of Multinational Enterprises: 1982–83.* London: Macmillan.

Stopford, John, John Dunning and Klaus Haberich. 1980. *The World Directory of Multinational Enterprises.* New York: Facts on File.

Strong, Norman, and Martin Walker. 1987. *Information and Capital markets.* New York: Basil Blackwell.

———. 1993. The explanatory power of earnings for stock returns. *The Accounting Review* 68:385-399.

Talmor, Eli. 1981. Asymmetric information, signaling, and optimal corporate financial decisions. *Journal of Financial and Quantitative Analysis* 16, no. 4 (November): 413–435.

Tang, Ming-je, and Chow-ming Joseph Yu. 1990. Foreign Market Entry: Production-related strategies. *Management Science* 36 (April): 476–489.

Teece, David. 1981a. The market for know-how and the efficient international transfer of technology. *Annals of the American Political and Social Science* 458: 81–96.

———. 1981b. The multinational enterprise: Market failure and market power consideration. *Sloan Management Review* 22 (Spring): 3–17.

———. 1983. Technological and organizational factors in the theory of multinational enterprise. In *Growth of International Business,* edited by Mark Casson. London: Allen and Unwin.

———. 1985. Multinational enterprise, internal governance, and industrial organization. *American Economic Review* 75, no. 2: 233–237.

———. 1986. Transactions cost economics and the multinational enterprise: An assessment. *Journal of Economic Behavior and Organization* 7: 21–45.

Telesio, Piero. 1979. *Technology Licensing and Multinational Enterprises.* New York: Praeger.

Theofilopoulou, Anna. 1989. Disclosure of information on FDI in the United States. *The CTC Reporter* no. 29 (Spring): 54–56.

Tsurumi, Yoshihiro. 1977. *Multinational Management: Business Strategy and Government Policy.* Cambridge, Mass.: Bollinger.

United Nations Center on Transnational Corporations (UNCTC). 1978. *Transnational Corporations in World Development: A Re-Examination.* New York: United Nations Publications.

———. 1987. *Transnational Corporations and Technology Transfer: Effects and Policy Issues.* New York: United Nation Publications.

———. 1988. *Transnational Corporations in World Development: Trends and Prospects.* New York: United Nation Publications.

———. 1995. *The World Investment Report 1995: Transnational Corporations and Competitiveness.* United Nations Publication.

U.S. Department of Commerce. *Survey of Current Business,* various issues. Washington, D.C.

Varian, Hal R. 1984. *Microeconomic Analysis.* New York: W. W. Norton & Co.

Vaupel, James. 1971. Characteristics and motivations of the U.S. corporations which manufacture abroad. Quoted in J. Dunning, The determinants of international production. *Oxford Economic Papers* 25, no. 3 (1973): 317.

Vernon, Ray. 1966. International investment and international trade in the product cycle. *Quarterly Journal of Economics* (May): 190–207.

———. 1971. *Sovereignty at Bay: The Multinational Spread of US Enterprise.* New York: Basic Books.

———. 1974. The location of economic activity. In *Economic Analysis and the Multinational Enterprise,* edited by J. Dunning. London: Allen & Unwin.

———. 1979. The product cycle hypothesis in a new international environment. *Oxford Bulletin of Economics and Statistics* (November): 255–267.

———. 1985. Comment on chapter by J. H. Dunning and G. Norman. In *Multinationals as Mutual Invaders,* edited by A. Erdilek. London: Croom Helm.

Williamson, Oliver. 1975. *Markets and Hierarchies: Analysis and Anti-trust Implications.* New York: Free Press.

———. 1981. The modern corporation: Origins, evolution, attributes. *Journal of Economic Literature* 19 (December): 1537–1568.

———. 1985. *The Economic Institutions of Capitalism.* New York: Free Press.

Wolf, B. M. 1977. Industrial diversification and internationalization: Some empirical evidence. *Journal of Industrial Economics* 26 (December): 177–191.

Index

About the Author

SCOTT X. LIU is a consultant for the World Bank and is actively involved in Chinese projects. He is also a consultant for several major Asian multinationals.

ISBN 0-275-95483-8

HARDCOVER BAR CODE